The
WISDOM
of
OZ

The WISDOM *of* OZ

USING PERSONAL ACCOUNTABILITY TO
SUCCEED IN EVERYTHING YOU DO

ROGER CONNORS and TOM SMITH

PORTFOLIO / PENGUIN

PORTFOLIO / PENGUIN
Published by the Penguin Group
Penguin Group (USA) LLC
375 Hudson Street
New York, New York 10014

USA | Canada | UK | Ireland | Australia | New Zealand | India | South Africa | China
penguin.com
A Penguin Random House Company

First published by Portfolio / Penguin, a member of
Penguin Group (USA) LLC, 2014

ISBN 978-1-59184-715-1

Printed in the United States of America
3 5 7 9 10 8 6 4 2

Set in Minion Pro
Designed by E. J. Strongin, Neuwirth & Associates, Inc.

CONTENTS

PREFACE

The Wisdom of Oz is not just a book about the power of personal accountability; it's a book about what's at the root of succeeding in everything you do. Simply put, when you unleash the power of personal accountability, it will empower you in life-altering ways. We're not talking fictional superhero-type powers but about a real, concrete power that enhances your ability to think, to withstand adversity, to generate confidence, and to increase your own natural emotional, mental, and intellectual strength to help you do what you need to do. We know this works because we've seen it in our own lives and witnessed it in the lives of countless others.

We first introduced this powerful accountability philosophy in our book *The Oz Principle*. Since then, millions have come to know us as "the Oz guys." Over the years we've helped leaders all over the world teach and apply the principles you're about to learn to those they work with, to generate billions of dollars of wealth—along with a host of even more important results. They got better results . . . a lot better results. And with those improvements they were able to dramatically impact their ability to deliver on their missions: such as bringing life-saving medications to market, improving education in community colleges, greatly surpassing charity fund-raising goals, and improving medical practices in battlefield hospitals.

You may not be looking to make any great changes in your life, but you may want to accomplish some great task—at least, a task that seems great to you. If this is the case, unleashing the power of personal accountability can be your best strategy. Our accountability philosophy is all about helping you accomplish what you want or need to do. *The Wisdom of Oz* will show you how others have done it and how you can do it too.

At the heart of the message lies this one simple truth: You can't let your circumstances define who you are and what you do. That kind of thinking only brings a sense of victimization that paralyzes your ability to think clearly, creatively, and quickly. Instead, you have to take accountability in order to take charge of shaping your circumstances. Do this and good things, positive things, game-changing things will begin to happen.

Easy to say, maybe harder to do.

To help bring these principles to life, we will share stories about people just like you who were able to overcome their challenges, like the New York–area fisherman who fell off his lobster boat and was adrift at sea for twelve hours in the chilly Atlantic . . . but survived. You will learn the traits that allowed a college senior, who fell flat on her face in a six-hundred-meter race, to jump up and win, or a thirteen-year-old soccer player to move from the bench to the starting lineup. You will discover that, while no one will ever wave a wizard's wand and magically solve all your problems, there is a way to experience the near-magical impact of personal accountability on what you want in life.

So why use the story of *The Wizard of Oz* to deliver the message? Because it is *the* story about the power that comes from taking personal accountability to deal with the circumstances you face. Dorothy, the Tin Man, the Scarecrow, and the Cowardly Lion all come to realize one important truth: no magic can give them what they want. In the end, they have to do it for themselves. We love their story and even suspect that author L. Frank Baum had the journey to greater accountability in mind when he first wrote *The Wonderful Wizard of Oz*.

The Wisdom of Oz lays out a clear path to unlocking the empowering influence of greater accountability in your own life. By the end you will feel more capable, more motivated, and more powerful. While you won't get many guarantees in life, you do get one here: The act of taking greater personal accountability, laid out in the pages ahead, will empower you to achieve what you most desire.

The
WISDOM
of
OZ

CHAPTER 1

If I Only Had a . . .

Dorothy: *The Wizard of Oz? Is he good or is he wicked?*

Glinda: *Oh, very good; but very mysterious. He lives in the Emerald City, and that's a long journey from here. Did you bring your broomstick with you?*

Dorothy: *No, I'm afraid I didn't.*

Glinda: *Well then, you'll have to walk. . . .*

Dorothy: *But how do I start for Emerald City?*

Glinda: *It's always best to start at the beginning. And all you do is follow the Yellow Brick Road.*

From the day L. Frank Baum's novel *The Wonderful Wizard of Oz* first appeared in 1900, it has captivated audiences around the world. Most of us have seen the iconic 1939 movie so many times that we know the story and songs by heart. Why do Dorothy, the Scarecrow, the Tin Man, and the Cowardly Lion touch us? Like all great entertainment, the story resonates. It hits home. We see ourselves in the characters and wish we possessed the power, the brains, the heart, and the courage to make our own dreams come true.

Think about what you want. What you really want. *If I only had a . . .* Is it a promotion or raise? Finding the love of your life? Improving a relationship? Rescuing a child? Saving a marriage? Getting a degree? Finding a new job? Making a difference in your community? Overcoming a persistent challenge or obstacle? We call the worthwhile things we want in life *results*, and this book is all about helping you get them. But they don't come easily.

Get Off the Couch!

On March 22, 2012, thirty-five days before the country's presidential elections, the Malian army stormed the presidential palace, overthrowing the western African country's twenty-year-old democracy. In the turmoil Islamic militants took control of two-thirds of the country and crushed Mali's democratic elections. "It was a tragic moment when the coup happened," says Yeah Samake, mayor of the small town of Ouélessébougou, located approximately forty miles from the chaos. "I came into my living room and completely collapsed on the couch. [Then] my wife came and kicked me. I couldn't believe it. I told her, 'I am looking for sympathy here. Why are you kicking me?' She only said, 'Get out there and go do something.'"

Whether you get off the couch on your own or require a little nudge from somewhere else, the point is to *get out there and go do something.* Mayor Samake's wife's kick gave him the resolve to get off the couch, get in the car, and drive through five rebel checkpoints into the heart of chaos. He soon found himself "in this military barrack with hundreds of nervous soldiers with guns." Mayor Samake's desire for a better life for his people emboldened him and propelled him through the troops to the coup leader, who demanded to know why he was there. Samake told him, "I have come to tell you that power does not belong in the hands of the military."

Impressed by his courage, the rebel leader, Captain Amadou Sanogo, invited Mayor Samake to speak to the Malian people on national television. Samake later did just that, denouncing the coup and demanding that power be restored to the people. Speaking from his heart, he added, "Change does not come from outside. It should come from within." Yeah Samake went on to become the democratic voice of his nation and made a real difference in the reinstatement of Mali's democratic presidential elections.

Rather than stay trapped by circumstances that seemed entirely beyond his control, Yeah Samake chose instead to be in control. He did what he could, rather than focusing on what he couldn't. That's the power of taking personal accountability. We call this The Wisdom of Oz:

Only you can unleash the positive power of personal accountability to overcome the obstacles you face and achieve the results you want.

Understanding the "big idea" of this book will help you tap into this power of personal accountability, but there will be more than one. Throughout *The Wisdom of Oz* we will be introducing related ideas that we call Oz Principles, which are foundational to making greater accountability work for you.

Controlling his circumstances rather than letting those circumstances control him is how it started with Mayor Samake and, as you will soon see, getting off the couch, dealing with your circumstances, and going after the result lies at the core of *The Wisdom of Oz*. You will also soon learn that while these principles of personal accountability are big enough to help you change the course of

> ## Oz Principle
>
> *When you can't control your circumstances, don't let your circumstances control you.*

—4—

history or the fate of a nation, they are also compact enough to help you improve any aspect of your personal life. It all comes down to what you really want and how badly you want it.

As you read *The Wisdom of Oz*, you will take the same journey of self-discovery that enabled Dorothy and her new friends to replace ignorance with knowledge, fear with courage, paralysis with power, and victimization with accountability. You will learn how to tap the inner power you already possess to get the results you want and to conquer any and all obstacles that get in your way.

No wizard can make that happen. Only you can do it. Sure, you may get a little help now and then, but your success depends largely on you. And just like the Scarecrow, the Tin Man, and the Cowardly Lion—who really wished they "only had a . . ."—you are going to discover the power that already lies within you to get what you're after. This book will show you how to harness that power, the power of your own personal accountability, and blow through any barriers that may have previously stood between you and success.

Now, we know the world is filled with fortune-tellers who gaze into their crystal balls while making all kinds of promises they can never keep. That's not who we are. That's not what you'll find in this book. We have spent decades researching and applying these principles to some of the toughest challenges the world can come up with. Without fail, these principles of greater personal accountability work, providing simple, powerful, and proven solutions. In the pages ahead you will read story after story of people who have applied this knowledge and developed the skills to get what they want.

It's actually pretty exciting to realize that desired results, better results, the results you want, lie within your reach and are not beyond your control. Of course, to get those results, you must get off the couch and do something about it. And while the couch seems like such a comfortable place to rest now and then, its warmth, security, and comfort may be the biggest enemy to your life's better results.

What is the couch for you? Is it a job that you really don't like but feels secure? Is it a longtime goal that you've never achieved? Is it a destructive relationship that you're afraid to change? How about a skill set that serves you well but that you need to drop in order to grow and get on with your life? Whatever it is, it's important to understand that most "breakthroughs" require a "break with." And that "break with" will most certainly mean leaving your comfort zone for the unknowns of your own yellow brick road.

Almost always, taking a step toward greater personal accountability to achieve the results you want requires a bold stroke on your part. Consider the comedic actor Jim Carrey, who grew up in a family so poor that at one point they lived in a van on a relative's lawn. But Carrey believed in his own future and in what he wanted to accomplish in his life. As the story goes, one night early in Carrey's struggling comic career, he drove his beat-up Toyota to the Hollywood Hills and, while sitting there overlooking Los Angeles, pulled out his checkbook and wrote himself a check for $10 million. He scribbled in the notation line, "For acting services rendered," and stuck it in his wallet. Carrey's bold stroke began with a pen and a fake check, with a personal resolve to take accountability and make it happen. Over the next five years, Jim Carrey's newfound belief in the result he desired led him to the worldwide success of *Ace Ventura*, *The Mask*, and *Liar Liar*. At the peak of his career, his per-film paycheck reached $20 million.

An incredible coincidence? Luck? Magic? Not for a second. His success was a testament to the power of personal accountability. And you don't have to be rich or famous to apply this. These principles can work for a family member, a neighbor, or you.

Take "Jenny," who came home one day to find a note from her husband saying their relationship was a lie and he was "letting her go." In the blink of an eye her once-loving husband's secret life turned hers upside down. The following months were horrible. Feeling depressed, unattractive, and withdrawn, she spent weeks hiding in her room. She became extremely uncomfortable in any social setting. When a friend finally talked her into attending a Halloween party after the divorce, she bought a costume and went, but it was a disaster. She just couldn't interact with other people, let alone flirt. So she left the party and started walking, eventually knocking on the door of a good friend who suggested it was time she make some real changes in her life, that she get back on track to her life-long goals of a happy marriage and family.

It wasn't easy, but Jenny took her friend's advice, and eventually her initial darkness, depression, and self-doubt gave way to hope and forward thinking, all because *she chose to change*. That decision finally pushed Jenny off her own version of the couch. Eventually, she bought a new car, colored her hair, found a new job, went back to school, and ran a half marathon, then another. Jenny says, "I came to realize that I was the only one who could improve my life." Today Jenny has the personal life she always wanted; she's beautiful, happy, and married to a great guy who loves her and treats her the way she deserves to be treated.

> ### Oz Principle
> *Every break "through" requires a "break with."*

Just like Jim Carrey, Yeah Samake, and Jenny, you really do have a say in how your life goes. What you are now learning will connect you to your true self and your own internal power, and it will help you see that you have the right, the ability, even the obligation to create your own best reality.

There Are No Wizards!

In *The Wizard of Oz* we meet Dorothy, the Scarecrow, the Tin Man, and the Cowardly Lion, who, through no fault of their own, find themselves in circumstances beyond their control. A tornado rips Dorothy from her Kansas farm and hurls her against her will to the Land of Oz. The Scarecrow lives a stagnant life amid corn and crows because his creator skimped on brains. The Tin Man is rusted in place, unable to act because he lacks the heart and will to move. And the tenderhearted Cowardly Lion, lacking courage and nerve, lives a life below his potential.

All of these timeless characters initially felt victimized by their shortcomings and circumstances. They believed they could not possibly change things on their own, so they set off on the yellow brick road to the Land of Oz in hopes of finding some all-powerful Wizard who would solve all of life's problems for them.

You remember the story. Arriving in the Emerald City after a treacherous journey, Toto, Dorothy's adorable little dog, pulls back the curtain to reveal a truly powerless Wizard, one who pulls levers and blows smoke but can do nothing for them.

A few key points:

1. Dorothy and her friends each knew exactly what they wanted: Kansas. A brain. A heart. Courage.

2. They each felt victimized, believing they could not control circumstances they had not themselves created.

3. They each needed to walk their own journey of discovery.

4. Each ultimately chose the path of greater personal accountability to get unstuck, overcome obstacles, and solve their problems.

In the pages ahead we will only lightly revisit the Oz story, but we'd like you to keep in mind how each of these characters eventually rose above their circumstances, their fear, their errant beliefs and shortcomings, to achieve their desired results. Getting what they wanted had nothing to do with the powerless Wizard and everything to do with their own powerful inner commitment to achieve their desired results. They conquered their challenges and fears and got what they wanted by working together, doing their best, and finding the power within.

Once you realize that nothing behind the curtain can help you get what you want in life, you will have discovered The Wisdom of Oz.

Today we live in a world where every day you hear that it's *other people* who are to blame for your condition. It's your parents. That mean teacher. A nosy neighbor. The government. An abusive husband. The ex-wife. Society. Prejudice.

Socioeconomic disparity. Your race. The president. God. Even your DNA. It's so easy to let yourself off the hook and blame someone or something else for your failure or inaction. It's so easy to believe that you are entitled to more, that someone else will solve your problems for you. This thinking is not true, not useful, and even downright dangerous.

You probably began reading this book because you want a better result or more success in some aspect of your life. We promise to help you achieve that. Over the last three decades we have seen these principles applied by people who are recognized as the world's best at what they do. As we mentioned earlier, these principles of personal accountability are big enough to fix the world's worst disasters yet intimate enough to repair what's going on within the walls of your own home. Application of the accountability principles taught in *The Wisdom of Oz* has preserved marriages, secured promotions at work, saved lives in the field of medicine and on the battlefields of Iraq and Afghanistan, helped athletes break records, aided students in nailing top grades, empowered church congregations to grow and flourish, enabled teachers to help students help themselves, revitalized businesses, and strengthened communities.

It's really exciting to consider that your wildest dreams can come true. So don't bury them. Don't dismiss them or ignore them. And please don't pretend they aren't there simply because you think you can no longer reach them.

Making the Choice

Greater accountability is a *choice*, perhaps the most powerful choice you can ever make. As with our friend Jenny, choosing accountability will empower you to overcome obstacles, beat challenges, and succeed in everything you do. Never forget that it's always a choice—your choice. A wise choice, a choice coupled with grit and commitment to all the hard work that acting on that choice entails.

> **OZ PRINCIPLE**
>
> *Greater accountability is the most powerful choice you will ever make.*

The remainder of this book will teach you how to consistently hone your own personal accountability skills in order to achieve your desired results. To help with this, we will introduce you to the Steps To Accountability—four commonsense steps designed to propel you along your journey to greater accountability and results.

Now, you might be thinking, *Yeah, this accountability stuff is nice and all, but there's a whole lot of bad things that happen to a whole lot of good people.* Well, in a sense you're right. A drunk driver plows into your car. A hurricane destroys your home. A bad economy triggers your layoff. None of it's your fault. It's really not. But how you react to these events is *your* responsibility. This is how you put the Oz Principles to work: by recognizing that you can't change yesterday but you can take charge of what happens today.

In the summer of 1981 John and Revé Walsh's six-year-old son, Adam, was abducted from a Florida department store. Sixteen days later authorities found his body. Like any loving parents, the Walshes grieved over such a horrific act of senseless brutality, but ultimately they did not succumb to victim thinking.

Ever since the murder of their son, John and Revé have worked tirelessly to battle criminal behavior. They founded the Adam Walsh Child Resource Center in four states, later merging their operation with the National Center for Missing and Exploited Children. They organized political campaigns and lobbied for a constitutional amendment for victims' rights. In spite of bureaucratic and legislative obstacles, John and Revé never gave up their cause, and their efforts eventually led to the creation of the Missing Children Act of 1982, the Missing Children's Assistance Act of 1984, and a law passed by the U.S. Congress in 2006 known as the Adam Walsh Child Protection and Safety Act. Many stores, malls, and major retailers such as Walmart, even began announcing a "Code Adam" when a child went missing from parents or family. You have probably seen the television program *America's Most Wanted*, which John hosted for over twenty years and which resulted in the arrest of more than 1,200 dangerous criminals.

Something bad happens; something good results. Accountability replaces victimhood. Failure gives way to success. It all starts with the Oz Principles.

What Do You Want?

So what do *you* want to accomplish with the tools offered on these pages? Financial and career success? A better body? An improved self-image? A position at the top of your class? Greater joy with friends and family? Think about a major result you want for yourself or a problem or obstacle blocking your progress. Write it down; carry it in your purse or wallet; tape it on a bathroom mirror. The more concrete and simple your goal, the better. For Yeah Samake it was democratic elections. For Jim Carrey, a $10 million dollar payday. For Jenny, a happy marriage and family. Don't overwhelm yourself by trying to change everything at once. Pick one thing, some specific goal, then apply what you are about to learn and watch it work.

With your feet set on the path to personal accountability, you will immediately begin to see these principles work for you as they empower you to change or deal with whatever has kept you from moving forward or stopped you from achieving success. Greater personal accountability, *The Wisdom of Oz* kind of accountability, will propel you toward the result you seek, helping you make it happen and achieve the results you want—results not magically provided by some wizard but earned by you.

The man behind the curtain is pulling levers and blowing smoke, but he can really do nothing for you. The power to succeed has always been within you.

CHAPTER 2
You Can't Go the Way You Came

Dorothy: *Oh, I'd give anything to get out of Oz altogether; but which is the way back to Kansas? I can't go the way I came!*

Glinda: *No, that's true. The only person who might know would be the great and wonderful Wizard of Oz himself.*

Here's some good news: To actually do what we are suggesting in this book won't cost you a penny. You won't need to go out and buy a new "this" or "that." You won't need a new personality or even a brain transplant. To implement the strategy of greater personal accountability and get the results you want, all you have to do is train yourself to *think differently,* to think accountably. Albert Einstein has been quoted as saying, "Insanity is doing the same thing over and over again and expecting different results." To get different results, better results, more results—you can't go the way you came. A new path forward is required and that's the path to greater personal accountability.

"Stuck on an Escalator" is a funny YouTube video that demonstrates the big impact of thinking differently. In the video a man and a woman are riding up an escalator, seemingly on their way to work. The escalator suddenly stops, leaving them stranded halfway to the second floor. The man mutters, "Oh, that's not good," while the exasperated woman says, "I don't need this." Neither of them has a phone, so they are stuck, alone in the building on a stalled escalator. The man reassures himself and the woman with the promise that "somebody will come," then yells in a panic, "Anybody out there?" More time passes until the woman eventually loses it, screaming, "Help!" while admitting she's going to cry. The man finally throws up his hands in exasperation and says, "There's nothing else left to do." So they just stand there, waiting on an escalator.

Do they really need someone else to bail them out? Do they really need any help at all? For the result they want—in this case, getting to the second floor—all they have to do is open their eyes, think differently, and walk up the escalator—which is, after all, just a set of stairs! Do you see how it's their perspective, their point of view, their belief that their circumstances are beyond their control that keeps these folks stuck and going nowhere while crying out for help?

Have you ever been "stuck on an escalator"?

Don't Be Afraid of Accountability

The solution to most of life's problems and opportunities is a strong dose of personal accountability. Tragically, however, people typically view accountability as something that happens *to* them when things go wrong. We realize that's a problem when it comes to our suggesting that greater personal accountability can be helpful to you.

Does the mere mention of the word "accountability" trigger your natural fight-or-flight instinct to run for cover in order to avoid the fallout you just know is coming? This negative and uninspiring view of accountability is reinforced in this common dictionary definition:

> **ac•count•a•bil•i•ty**
> *(noun)*
> Subject to having to report, explain, or justify; being answerable, responsible.

With a definition like this, no wonder people have problems accepting accountability. Being "subject to having to" do anything unpleasant clearly means something is about to happen *to* you. To our way of thinking, this old-school view of accountability explains a lot of what's wrong with accountability in the world today.

Over the years we have been amazed to see the lengths to which people will go to dodge their negative view of accountability. Consider these snippets from actual traffic accident reports provided by real, living, breathing adults explaining on an official public form why an accident happened:

- "Coming home, I drove into the wrong house and collided with a tree that I don't have."
- "The telephone pole was approaching fast. I was attempting to swerve out of its path when it struck my front."
- "I pulled away from the side of the road, glanced at my mother-in-law, and headed over the embankment."
- "The indirect cause of this accident was a little guy in a small car with a big mouth!"

Passing the buck, dodging the bullet, running for cover—that's the natural human reaction when it comes to the old textbook notion of accountability. Facing this kind of accountability, people just naturally resort to the avoidance strategies we human beings use to get off the hook, whether or not we were really ever on a hook at all.

You unleash the real power of personal accountability when accountability becomes something you do to yourself voluntarily to ensure success, not something you're forced to do to account for failure. While one component of accountability is feeling responsible for the outcomes of your actions, there is another even more important side, the side that empowers you to succeed. It's the secret sauce of success and something you should never fear.

> ## Oz Principle
> *Accountability is something you do to yourself.*

The Steps To Accountability

We call our secret sauce the Steps To Accountability. This new way of thinking is what personal accountability is all about. In the illustration on the next page you will notice a line separating Above The Line thinking from Below The Line thinking. Above The Line is where you take personal accountability to overcome obstacles and achieve the results you want to achieve. Here you take the steps to See It, Own It, Solve It, and Do It. The Steps To Accountability can have a magical effect on how you think and act.

Below The Line is where we can all get stuck in the blame game, focused on excuses rather than results. Here

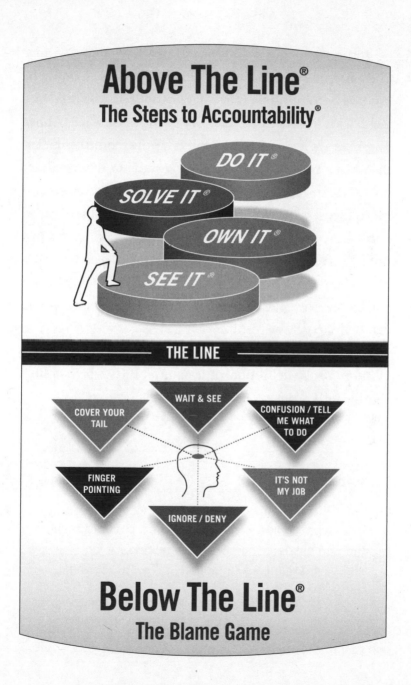

Above The Line®
The Steps to Accountability®

DO IT®

SOLVE IT®

OWN IT®

SEE IT®

THE LINE

WAIT & SEE

COVER YOUR TAIL

CONFUSION / TELL ME WHAT TO DO

FINGER POINTING

IT'S NOT MY JOB

IGNORE / DENY

Below The Line®
The Blame Game

—21—

obstacles seemingly outside our control can stop us. Above The Line we stay focused on what we can do. Below The Line we become blinded by all we cannot do and therefore feel frustrated with our inability to move forward. Above The Line we are looking for ways to overcome obstacles. Below The Line we are looking for people to remove those obstacles for us. Above The Line we feel less stressed and more focused. Below The Line we often get discouraged and whiny. It's not wrong to slip Below The Line; it's just not a useful place to spend your time. You need to recognize when you are there and then move as quickly as you can back Above The Line to get refocused on what else you can to do to get the results you want.

With the Steps To Accountability in mind, here's *The Wisdom of Oz* definition of accountability, which differs significantly from what you're probably used to:

The
WISDOM
of
OZ

ac·count·a·bil·i·ty
(noun)

A personal choice to rise above one's circumstances and demonstrate the ownership necessary for achieving desired results: to See It, Own It, Solve It, and Do It.

Dennis, a very successful sales vice president of a medical device company and a believer in Above The Line accountability, received a phone call informing him that his company would have no new products to sell for the third year in a row. Three years with nothing new to sell! Now, this might have been okay if he could just slack off, go golfing, and coast for another year until the company came up with something new, but the company still expected Dennis and his sales guys to hit the same big numbers.

If you were Dennis, what would you be thinking? What would you be worried about? Your job, your wife, your kids, your house payments, your sanity, your future, the jobs of those who work for you? All of the above?

Before Dennis could get his mind around what was going on, the phone rang and it was both his East Coast and West Coast sales managers: "Dennis, we gotta meet!" Within hours the three of them were sitting in a St. Louis airport lounge for an emergency meeting, where the first words out of the managers' mouths were "Dennis, can we go Below The Line for a few minutes?" After all, anyone in this situation would certainly be justified in feeling the victim and taking a quick trip Below The Line.

Dennis set his watch alarm for thirty minutes, and off they went, venting, moaning, and groaning about a whole list of things that were clearly outside their control: They were being victimized again by product development. They didn't deserve it. Why was this happening to them again? Before they knew it, ding-ding-ding! The alarm went off. The thirty minutes were gone. In a moment of suspense, the two managers looked at Dennis, wondering if he would really shift the conversation and move everyone Above The Line. Though their little excursion Below The Line had cleared their minds a bit and freed some pent-up emotions, Dennis knew staying down there would accomplish little. So he sighed, quickly smiled, and said, "Okay, let's get Above The Line now." And they did, just like that. For the next forty-five minutes they moved through the Steps To Accountability to See It, Own It, Solve It, and Do It.

So what were their results? Without going into all the details, not only did they come up with creative solutions to their problem, their results were off the charts. In spite of a third year with no new products, they turned in a record sales performance. When Dennis was asked how they did it, he simply said, "We had no new products and no new people, just a new way of looking at the problem— an Above The Line way." They had every reason to play the victim and blame others, but instead they changed their thinking by choosing to focus on what they *could* do, rather than on what they could not do. That produced some creative Above The Line thinking to overcome some pretty big obstacles.

The point of this story is that moving Above The Line is a choice—a powerful choice that brings new options

and new opportuni-
ties. If we drop Below
The Line, we need to
know it and then work
to get back Above The
Line as soon as we can.

Oz Principle

It's not wrong to go Below The Line; it's just not effective to stay there.

The rest of this book will help you learn how to apply Above The Line thinking just as consciously as Dennis and, in the same way, take the Steps To Accountability to See It, Own It, Solve It, and Do It. For now, just see that Below The Line is home to all the old blaming, excuse-making, and they-made-me-do-it behaviors. Above The Line thinking is accountability thinking. It's the kind of thinking that allows you to take the steps to rescue your-self from the escalator, rather than stand there waiting for someone else to come along and do it for you—which, by the way, may never happen.

And what about the line itself? It's really just that men-tal hurdle we all must consciously and consistently stay above in order to be accountable. It sounds simple, but in a world that sometimes feels as though it is dead set on pulling us down, it's those who can consciously and con-sistently stay Above The Line who win.

It's a choice to think differently about your circum-stances and about the things you cannot control versus those you can. This new thinking will lead to new solu-tions, new avenues, and new strategies for succeeding.

Life Is Always Better Above The Line

In light of all the very real promises we're making, it's important to realize that the Steps To Accountability only work if you become personally accountable for how you *think* and *act*. The goal is to consistently think Above The Line.

As you read this, you're only human if you're thinking about all the other people in your life who you believe block your ability to get what you want. All those who are Below The Line in their own lives and how they rub off on you. Those who may even stand as obstacles to you and your ability to achieve the result you most want. If you're thinking all this, we simply ask, who is the most important person in your life who needs to be Above The Line? Obvious answer: you! As Socrates once said, "Let him that would move the world first move himself."

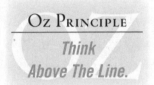

Oz Principle

Think Above The Line.

To demonstrate how these principles work in even the simplest and most common of circumstances, consider the story of a thirteen-year-old girl's Seattle-area soccer team. The team had recently moved from a recreational league to a competitive league—something new to the girls. Given the new situation, not everyone would get an equal turn to play, as they had in the past. Every player now had to earn her spot.

Their coach, Jared, recalls that one day at the beginning of a game early in the season, one of the three players who consistently sat on the bench, "Jessie," got his attention and asked, "Why am I always on the bench at the start of the game?" He confessed surprise, then responded bluntly, "Well, you aren't as good as they are," referring to her fellow players out on the field. Jessie was dumbfounded. *"What?!"* He went on to tell her, "You aren't as good as they are. If you want to play at the beginning then get better and take one of their spots."

Jared eventually put Jessie in the game and, he says, "she instantly played lights out. She was like a whole different player—all over the place, jumping into plays, taking balls—nothing like she used to be." When Jessie ran off the field after a phenomenal game, she came right up to him and asked, "Did I earn a starting position, Coach?" His answer? "Absolutely!"

So how did that happen? How did Jessie go from a lackluster player to a future superstar? She changed her thinking. Then her thinking changed her actions.

Picture this bench-warming young woman, utilizing a fraction of her potential, blaming her coach and other players for her lack of opportunity and probably feeling like a Below The Line victim. The reality? It was all about what was going on inside her own head. All along, Jessie had had all this pent-up talent and potential just waiting to explode. After she worked up the courage to ask her coach that key question—"Why am I always on the bench?"—Jessie used his painful answer to change her thinking. After she got her head right, she was really able to start pounding on the potential that was in her all the time. The same is true for you, and your results can be just as dramatic.

> **Oz Principle**
>
> *You must be personally accountable for how you think and act.*

What makes some people crumble under hardship or adversity and stay "on the bench" while others soar above their circumstances? Jessie certainly could have played it safe and hunkered down Below The Line on the bench feeling sorry for herself. But she wanted more; she wanted her coach to put her in the game. The result completely changed her soccer experience as a youth and most likely her life going forward.

Now, it's probably obvious that Jessie had not read this book just yet, so what caused her to act Above The Line? Jessie did what most people do when success is the outcome; she made the intuitive choice to take accountability and not be victimized by her situation. She took control of her circumstances, rather than have her circumstances control her. Jessie chose to act rather than be acted on. That's the essence of what it means to move Above The Line.

As we will come to see, Above The Line thinking means abandoning a victim's "I'm on the bench because of them" mentality. It requires you to be responsible for you and shift zero blame elsewhere. The buck consistently stops in the mirror. Not so easy to do, but possible.

Now, there are a whole lot of us who carry around emotional baggage regarding our time "on the bench." One of the authors has seared into his memory his literal time on the bench, at age ten in Pony League baseball. At one point the coach replaced him on second base with another player—a guy who had a broken arm and was wearing a cast on his throwing hand! Yeah, it seems funny now, but not so much at the time. It became clear later that a little favoritism was going on, but even before that, those close to the situation knew this young man wasn't riding the bench for lack of trying. More than once he was tempted to join another benchwarmer, who simply walked away in the middle of a game and never came back. But he didn't want to quit. So rather than surrender to circumstances that were out of his control, he chose to "stay in the game," even if it meant warming the bench with his backside.

The reality is, you won't always get what you want. In this case, though the author never went on to play for the New York Yankees, he did enjoy the fame and fortune (in his mind, anyway) of Colt League, the division just above

Pony. And he learned a real lesson: not to give up. He learned to endure unfairness and not to wallow in self-pity or quit. These little building blocks of experience early in life showed him that operating Above The Line is always the best course of action. Always.

Choose to Get Above The Line

Back in chapter 1 we asked you to think about a result you wanted to achieve. If you haven't already done so, do it now. It may be something like:

- Become a better parent and enjoy the role more
- Get promoted faster at work
- Finish school
- Overcome a major challenge or setback with health, weight, job, or financial loss
- Gain some athletic ability or accomplish some athletic feat (a marathon, etc.)
- Feel happier, with less stress and frustration, less disappointment, and more capacity to deal with adversity
- Attain a better job or find one you love if you're currently out of work
- Become more social

- Get more involved in your church group or community
- Enjoy a more abundant lifestyle
- Experience greater overall success and quality of life
- Obtain all the benefits of a more fulfilling marriage

You might be tempted to mock a list like this and the idea that we believe accountability can "magically" fix so many things. Fair enough. A little healthy skepticism is okay; just know that we've seen these principles work millions of times over the past twenty years.

Dorothy easily could have stayed in Munchkinland, where she was instantly adored. She would have been a celebrity, praised—even worshipped. But being queen of the Munchkins wasn't what she wanted for herself. She wanted to return to Kansas and knew she couldn't go back the way she had come—she had to find another way. A new way. The Scarecrow could also have remained content to sit in a field getting pecked at by crows, but he wanted more. So did the Tin Man and the Cowardly Lion. Wanting a better you is a good thing.

The
WISDOM
of
OZ

It's not about what you do; it's about how you think.

For a different result . . . think differently.

Think Above The Line.

CHAPTER 3

LIONS AND TIGERS AND BEARS, OH MY!

Scarecrow: *Uh! Oh, this is terrible! Can't budge her an inch! This is a spell, this is!*

Tin Man: *It's the Wicked Witch! What'll we do? Help! Help!*

Scarecrow: *It's no use screaming at a time like this! Nobody will hear you! Help! Help! Help!*

Everyone knows Murphy's Law: "If anything can go wrong, *it will.*" During a trip to Ireland we learned of O'Reilly's corollary: "Murphy was an optimist!" In other words, when difficult obstacles present themselves and things go wrong, they often go *really* wrong.

When that happens it is only human nature to fall Below The Line into the trap of the victim cycle and play the blame game. It's not wrong to be there; it's just not productive, because nothing much good happens Below The Line. Problems don't get solved, goals aren't attained, and dreams die. Down there it's also easy to duck responsibility and blame everyone and everything else when you aren't succeeding. Sure, you can get some sympathy; you may even get off the hook, at least temporarily. But real results? Forget it.

Here's a creative solution to accountability ducking that has made its way across the Internet from Australia to North America—something a high school staff in California reportedly concocted and wished they could have put on their school telephone answering machine:

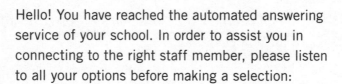

Hello! You have reached the automated answering service of your school. In order to assist you in connecting to the right staff member, please listen to all your options before making a selection:

- To lie about why your child is absent, press 1.

- To make excuses for why your child did not do his work, press 2.

- To complain about what we do, press 3.

- To swear at staff members, press 4.

- To ask why you didn't get information that was already enclosed in your newsletter and several flyers mailed to you, press 5.

- If you want us to raise your child, press 6.

- If you want to reach out and touch, slap, or hit someone, press 7.

- To request another teacher for the third time this year, press 8.

- To complain about bus transportation, press 9.

- To complain about school lunches, press 0.

- If you realize this is the real world and your child must be accountable and responsible for his/her own behavior, classwork, and homework, and that it's not the teacher's fault for your child's lack of effort, hang up and have a nice day!

The whole idea apparently came about because the charter school administration tried to implement a policy with the crazy expectation that students and parents would accept accountability for the children's absences and missing homework. But the school and teachers were threatened with lawsuits by parents who wanted their children's failing grades changed to passing grades—

even though their kids were absent far more times than attendance policies permitted. To our knowledge a recording like this never went live, but we bet the faculty wished it had.

I'm a victim. I didn't do it. I'm not responsible. They made me do it. They didn't do it for me. The dog ate my homework. Is it possible that more and more people are ducking accountability because society today enables it, supports it, even promotes it? It seems we live in a world where people increasingly shun accountability and treat victimhood and blaming as perfectly acceptable alternatives.

> **OZ PRINCIPLE**
>
> *Nothing much good happens Below The Line.*

When Bob Filner, former mayor of San Diego, was accused of sexual harassment, his initial response was to deny that he had done anything wrong. Then he blamed the women who had brought the accusations against him for being too "uptight," claiming they were overreacting and that it was their fault for "misinterpreting" his "fun-loving" nature. Then, finally, when the tide of public opinion began to shift against the mayor and evidence piled up, with more and more witnesses coming forward, he started pointing fingers and called himself "the victim of a lynch mob." When that didn't work, in a desperate final attempt to push accountability elsewhere, he blamed the appalling way he treated women on how he was raised, insinuating (in the words of one reporter) that "he'd been a captive of a sexist '50s culture. *Not really my fault. I'm just so old.*"

As allegations continued to mount and when more than twenty women had come forward, Below The Line Bob found himself backed into a corner and was forced to face reality. Only then did he publicly admit his wrongdoing, saying, "The behavior I have engaged in over many years is wrong. My failure to respect women and the intimidating conduct I engaged in at times is inexcusable." Ironically, this from a man who had exhausted every possible excuse. Then, nearly in his next breath, he demonstrated that nothing had changed: He and his legal team blamed the city for not having provided sexual harassment training—arguing that San Diego should therefore pay his legal fees. It didn't.

Ultimately forced to resign in disgrace, Filner received many "parting gifts," including a mirror from famed attorney Gloria Allred, who said that Bob could "look at [it] when asking who's to blame for his resignation." Despite all the despicable and ugly things the mayor may have done, he did gain something really valuable: an invitation to take a long, honest look in the mirror.

Rules of the Blame Game

Go ahead, blame someone. Everyone does it. Sometimes it even works. But if you're going to do it, you should do it right. Here are six tongue-in-cheek rules for playing the blame game. They sum up thousands of years of human experience with finger-pointing and excuse making:

- **Rule #1: Never blame someone who offers a better excuse than you.** This is the cardinal mistake and one only a novice would make. It's blame-game musical chairs out there, and you don't want to be the last one standing when the music stops.

- **Rule #2: Always be prepared to pass the buck, pin the blame, or point the finger, particularly when it's really your fault.**

- **Rule #3: Remember, a good excuse can be just as good as getting the result.** We've all experienced this: we get off the hook with an off-the-charts great story. Or when we don't produce results, we at least supply good, compelling reasons. And when those reasons truly are compelling, it can be just as good as getting the result.

- **Rule #4: The quality of an excuse increases proportionately with the degree to which the "reason" lies outside

your control. This rule speaks to the quality of the story we tell. Of course, the best stories should work in every circumstance by relying on such proven excuses as the weather, the economy, the government, an ex-spouse . . . The list goes on. So much to blame, so little time!

- **Rule #5: Turn to the standard "scapegoat" excuses when normal deflecting tactics aren't working.** These excuses are the ones that have become acceptable to pull out of the hat at just the right moment, so that everyone will nod in agreement. Like these we've probably all used when getting to work late: *My alarm didn't go off. The traffic was bad. Someone didn't fill up the car with gas. I couldn't find my keys.*

- **Rule #6: When all else fails, admit your guilt but blame your childhood.**

The lesson we should all learn is that all the "blame-storming" in the world will never move you closer to the success you want. And though today's lawsuit-happy society tries to convince us of the true value of faultfinding and blame shifting, it actually exacts a terrible price by robbing us of the one thing we can do for ourselves: take accountability.

The solution? Children need to stop blaming parents, students and parents must stop blaming teachers and schools, drunks should stop blaming the bottle and cigarette smokers the cigarette, overweight fast-food addicts should stop pointing fingers at the burger makers, and bad people ought to stop blaming the devil. Finding convenient reasons to shift responsibility or blame is never healthy and never brings better results.

Now, this doesn't mean there aren't legitimate victims, because there are. Every day bad people do horrible things and good people get hurt and suffer great tragedy. It's also hard to turn on the news without hearing about some manmade or natural disaster or misfortune. In such cases the injured have every right to remain victims as long as they like. No one would deprive them of those feelings. In fact, we can and should offer sympathy and a helping hand whenever we can. Yet all victims must ultimately decide how long they will stay stuck in their suffering. No one can put a clock on when people are ready to end the victimhood and move to a better place. In the end it's still a choice, though a difficult one.

> **Oz Principle**
>
> *Playing the blame game never brings better results. Never.*

What It Means to Be Below The Line

So what does it mean to be Below The Line? It simply means to have a mind-set that allows you to stay stuck, a victim of your circumstances. When you live Below The Line, you externalize your lack of progress toward the result you want or your failure to solve the problem you face. To reside Below The Line means you have stopped trying to overcome the obstacles and have decided that the solution lies beyond you, out of your control, that someone else will need to solve the problem for you. Remember the escalator from chapter 2?

The gravitational tug from Below The Line is ever constant because the obstacles and challenges keeping us from what we want are real and often very hard to solve. It is the reality of these issues that makes going Below The Line so attractive and easy. Because they are real issues, they legitimize the idea that we are stuck: *Surely, everyone can see that I am justified in feeling this way.*

Six Stages of the Victim Cycle

To help further define Below The Line victimhood, we have, over the years, boiled down the many victim-cycle and blame-game excuses into six major categories. It's important that you become familiar with each so you can recognize when you or those close to you get caught up in it.

Ignore/Deny

If you ignore a toothache, pretend a leaky pipe will fix itself, or deny there are weeds in your yard, what happens? Right: a root canal, a flooded basement, and the prettiest dandelion farm in three counties. Similarly, if you bury your head in the sand and remain stuck Below The Line, life only gets worse. Just ask the lowly ostrich. According to experts at the San Diego Zoo, "when an ostrich senses danger and cannot run away, it flops to the ground and remains still, with its head and neck flat out in front of it. Because the head and neck are lightly colored, they blend in with the color of the soil. From a distance, it just looks like the ostrich has buried its head in the sand." Neither burying your head nor flopping to the ground and playing dead is a decent option. So get yourself to your dentist, patch the leak, and grab a hoe.

It's Not My Job

While visiting a local restaurant, we saw a number of employees enjoying their break. Burgers and fries done and break over, they were joking and shoving one another when one of them spilled his tray. Garbage and fry sauce hit the floor. This got a big laugh as everyone walked off, leaving the kid to stand there over his mess. We then heard him say, word for word, "It's not my job." Laughing, he walked off to join his buddies, leaving the floor for somebody else. Now, this might not seem like a big deal to you, but it's a symptom of something huge, not just for this restaurant but for society in general. There is a pervasive lack of ownership out there, a widespread lack of personal integrity; the buck is passed from one person to another to another. Though you may think you are getting away with something, ducking responsibility will, in the end, only paralyze your life and keep you from getting any real results. From now on, when you see a mess, pick it up, especially if you're the one who made it in the first place.

Finger-pointing

"Bradley" recently told his wife that, after many years of struggle, he has come to the conclusion that he's "meant to be miserable so there's no sense fighting it." For years he has cycled through disabling depression, an unhappy marriage, a lackluster career, financial trials, struggling children, and an unfulfilled life. Through it all he has tried psychology, psychiatry, medication, religion, lack of religion, and just about anything else he and others in his circle of friends think might help. His conclusion? "It's heredity." Armed with that trusty diagnosis, he now points the finger of blame at his parents. To compound the situation, his once-capable wife now feeds his victim frenzy by also piling on his parents. How would you fix Bradley?

What would you tell him? Perhaps Bradley could borrow ex-mayor Bob Filner's mirror.

Confusion/Tell Me What to Do

A lot of people think confusion lets them off the hook. When the soup hits the floor, the kids say, "I don't know where Mom keeps the mop." The dishwasher needs to be emptied. "I can't reach the cupboard, so I can't put the dishes away." The lawnmower runs out of gas. "I don't know where Dad keeps the gas can." So it's back to video games. Confusion reigns. Accountability wanes. And another "tell me what to do" victim qualifies for the victim cycle hall of shame. Confusion is the great defender of the status quo. Nothing and no one will ever change when we get lost in the swamps of confusion and "tell me what to do."

Cover Your Tail

We all do it. No one wants something bad to be their fault, and everyone has a story ready about why it's not. The phenomenon is everywhere. Turn to any page of the paper or watch any news channel and you'll quickly find examples. ABC News ran a story entitled MEXICAN TEXTBOOKS RIDDLED WITH ERRORS. It revealed that 235 million school textbooks had been printed with the kinds of mistakes teachers expect their students to avoid: misspellings, grammatical and punctuation errors, geographical blunders, etc. No sooner did the news get out than the tail covering began. The Mexican education secretary called the errors "unforgivable" and blamed Mexico's "previous administration." The head of the Education Commission protected himself by blaming the books' editors. The editors chalked up the errors to their low pay. And so it goes. Oh, did you catch the fact that they had printed 235 *million* books? That's a lot of tail covering.

Wait and See

Imagine yourself standing in the path of a roaring wall of water. Hurricane Katrina is hurtling toward your town and you're told to evacuate immediately. What would you do? Would you leave or move to higher ground? Would you sit on your front porch, waiting to see if the wind and water would sweep you away? Sadly, during Katrina, rescuers needed to evacuate thousands of people who had heard the news but chose to stick around to *wait and see.* We all know the Katrina story; for every person who joined the difficult evacuation, another ten ignored the warnings and stood waiting. A writer friend of ours likes to say, "Do something, even if it's wrong." Action, any action, produces more results than paralysis ever will.

Stuck Below The Line

Many people spend so much time Below The Line, trudging around the victim cycle, that it becomes a habit. They aren't happy unless they are moaning about this problem or that bad news, blaming this or that person, pretending confusion, or playing some other woe-is-me self-pity victim game. Underlying all these excuses is the reality that people can find so much comfort in crying victim that, without realizing it, they literally start trading sympathy from others for their own success. Whatever sympathy they can solicit becomes their paycheck. At first glance this seems ludicrous, but we've all done it.

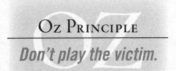

Oz Principle

Don't play the victim.

Some time ago we were asked to speak with "Kevin," an eighteen-year-old whose family was concerned about him. Kevin had seen two different medical specialists; one diagnosed him with autism and the other who said he was fine and didn't have it. No one knew for sure whether Kevin really was suffering from autism or not. Despite this, Kevin persisted in telling everyone he had it. At one point in our conversation, we stopped him and flatly asked, "Do you *want* to have autism?" Somewhat shocked, he said, "No." We asked, "If you have been told you may or may not have autism, and you don't want to have it, then why are you telling people you do have it?" The look on his face showed that he hadn't thought about this before. We then suggested, "Given the fact that the specialists can't agree on whether you have autism or not, you have a choice in your life that most people in this situation don't have. You get to choose."

Making a choice was an option Kevin had never considered. We went on to say, "If you choose not to have it, then you also have to be willing to *give up any sympathy* you have been getting by telling people that you have it. You can no longer play the victim. Are you ready to do that?" He answered firmly, "Yes, this is what I want!" We urged him never to claim autism again, unless it was conclusively established and became medically necessary.

Now, we aren't saying Kevin's case is typical, and we aren't doctors or therapists, but for Kevin whether he truly had autism or not wasn't the point. The point was that he could give up playing the victim and move forward in his life with newfound confidence. Though it's hard for many to grasp, all of us really do choose whether to think and act like a victim of our circumstances. Or not.

Time for *You* to Rise Above The Line

This is what *The Wisdom of Oz* is all about: guiding you through a concrete, step-by-step process of shedding victimhood and becoming a results-driven, accountable, and vibrant person. Dorothy and her three friends learned to shed victim cycle thinking and take the powerful steps necessary to beat the witch and reach their dreams—dreams that had very little to do with wizards, rainbows, or ruby slippers and a lot to do with their own thinking, choices, and Above The Line actions. You can do the same.

So just how do you leave the victim cycle? Just how do you shed Below The Line thinking and behavior? You keep what you want firmly in mind and *choose* to rise Above The Line by learning to consistently See It, Own It, Solve It, and Do It—our four Steps To Accountability. As we said before, this isn't easy, but it is possible when you're armed with a working knowledge of these four Above The Line steps—steps you are now prepared to learn how to use.

Nothing much good happens
Below The Line: problems don't get solved,
goals aren't attained, and dreams die.

CHAPTER 4

The Cowardly Lion: Mustering the Courage to See It

Dorothy: *Why, you're nothing but a great big coward.*

Cowardly Lion: *You're right, I am a coward. I haven't any courage at all. I even scare myself. Look at the circles under my eyes. I haven't slept in weeks.*

Tin Man: *Why don't you try counting sheep?*

Cowardly Lion: *That doesn't do any good, I'm afraid of them.*

Seeing the world as it really is takes courage. Most of us think we are generally right about things. We see the world through our own lens and what we see is "the way it is." As Mark Twain reportedly said, "It's not what you don't know that gets you into trouble, it's what you know for sure that just ain't so." The modern-day version of Twain's insight can be found in a line from the film *Men in Black*, when Agent K, speaking about aliens living among us, says, "Fifteen hundred years ago everybody knew the earth was the center of the universe. Five hundred years ago everybody knew the earth was flat. And fifteen minutes ago you knew that humans were alone on this planet." Because we all hold on pretty tightly to what we know, even if it ain't so, you will likely find the See It step the most difficult of all the Steps To Accountability.

How do you see things as they really are? How do you work up the courage to admit *your* reality may not actually be *the* reality? As with everything related to accountability, it all starts with making a personal choice. Irena Sendler made that choice.

The Nazis invaded Poland on September 1, 1939. Three and a half years later, Warsaw's Jewish population had dropped by nearly 90 percent, from 450,000 to 55,000, as most of Poland's Jewish community had been killed or sent to death camps. What would you do if you were a twenty-nine-year-old Polish Catholic social worker living on the "safe side" of the nine-foot ghetto wall? Every day you walk among the Jewish people and witness what is happening to your neighbors. You also know what the Nazis would do to you should you try to intervene. Since you're not Jewish, it's just better to keep your head down, play it safe, and mind your own business.

This was Irena Sendler, eyes open but not really seeing. She was like most of us, who half notice the homeless or others in need around us but don't really *see* them. Then one day in the ghetto, Irena found herself looking into the desperate eyes of a starving child, and everything changed. In those eyes was something that reminded her of advice her deceased father used to give: "You see a man drowning, you must try to save him, even if you cannot swim." That was the day Irena went from living in her *own* reality to seeing *the* reality.

In spite of her mother's pleas, Irena started passing herself off as a nurse so she could slip under the Germans' noses. Moving through the ghetto from one Jewish door to another, she started convincing Jewish mothers to let her take their children to safety. She and her friends eventually smuggled 2,500 Jewish children to freedom in toolboxes, suitcases, potato sacks, and coffins. They sedated babies or taped their mouths shut to keep them quiet. They got them out through sewers and secret basement tunnels. When the Nazis finally figured out what was going on and captured Irena, they tortured her, fracturing both her legs, and sentenced her to death. Miraculously, a bribed guard let her escape.

Thousands are alive today because one courageous woman chose to see. This is the power of

Oz Principle

See things as they really are.

taking the See It step and acknowledging reality. This is the power of personal accountability. The power of achievement. The power that can change your life and the lives of everyone around you.

Seeing the Whole Picture

Almost everyone has experienced the surprise that comes when you get a new car and then begin to notice something you had not noticed before: It seems like every other driver is in the same kind of car you are! Psychologists call this sudden ability to See It selective perception, which is their way of saying that we see what we are familiar with.

To demonstrate, let's run a small experiment. On the following page is a picture. In just a minute we're going to ask you to turn the page and check it out, making a mental note of as many different objects as you can—but you only get four seconds to look at it. Are you ready? Go ahead and turn the page—remember, only four seconds.

What did you see? How many images do you remember? A baby? A panda? A cruise ship? If you are like most people, in the limited time allowed you will remember only four or five images. Why did you see only a few and miss the rest?

It is human nature to "lock in" on what you are familiar with and "block out" everything else, which is what happened with the picture exercise you just completed. This lock-in/block-out reflex produces blind spots that limit your ability to solve problems, improve relationships, overcome obstacles, and get the results you want. When you're driving, for example, it can be deadly not to check your blind spots before changing lanes. Just because you don't see a car doesn't mean it's not there. To make sure, you have to make a special effort to check your mirrors and look over your shoulder.

When it comes to our ability to See It, we all have blind spots that give us a distorted view of reality, allowing us to see only part of the picture—that part of the picture we are already familiar with. Yet as in the picture exercise, just because you did not see something does not mean it wasn't there.

It is nearly impossible to take accountability and successfully navigate the See It step when you don't have a full view of what you're really facing. You can't be accountable for what you don't know or, in this case, what you cannot see. So that means you have to look smart and hard, so you can See

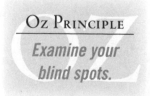

Oz Principle

Examine your blind spots.

It. The more you improve your ability to See It, the more successful will be your journey Above The Line.

Why People Fail to See It

The cost of not seeing something can be huge. Take, for example, a man we'll call "Luis Alvarez," a successful businessman, husband, and father—or so he thought until the day he walked in the door from another long day at work to find his wife and two young children standing there in coats, bags packed. As his family drove away in tears, leaving him alone in the driveway, Luis remembers feeling blindsided and in total shock. It turns out Luis had not seen the entire picture; he hadn't heard his wife complain for many years about his continual absence and what it was doing to his marriage, home, and family.

Luis admits to spending days, weeks, and even months after his family left feeling angry and frustrated, making all the usual excuses for problems that weren't his fault: *She didn't talk to me. She didn't come to me. I was doing all I was doing for her and the kids. It's her. It's them. How ungrateful! If my boss didn't make me work so much* . . . Why didn't Luis see that his workaholic schedule was harming his family until it was too late? The same reason many of us have trouble seeing these same things in our own lives: Blind spots prevent us from seeing the whole picture.

Seeing It often has just as much do to with your ears as it does with your eyes. At times we just need to tune in and start hearing the perspectives of those around us in order to see the entire picture.

In Luis's case, after months of frustration and pain over the slow realization that his wife and kids were never coming back, something changed. He remembers one day noticing, taped to the wall in his office, a little printout showing our Steps To Accountability. He remembered then that he had attended one of our classes and knew this stuff. Luis was stunned—had this reminder of accountability really been right there in front of him for a whole year? He says, "It's like my eyes just opened. I remembered the chart and having learned about the steps. I thought about my ex-wife and kids and how miserable I was. I had made life worse by being a victim, drowning in all the excuses and all the stuff that I felt was happening to me."

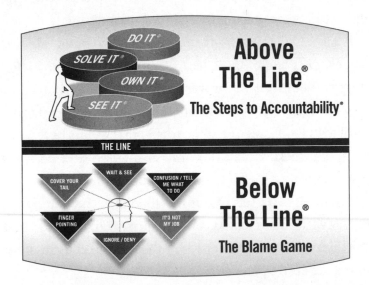

After taking time to internalize the Steps To Accountability and think about how they applied to his situation, Luis realized how far Below The Line he was living and how long he'd been down there. He remembers asking himself, *What do I really need to see here?* And that was it.

The blinders dropped; his eyes opened. Only then could he see the reality of the situation. "I had put this all on my wife for her leaving, but there were a

> **OZ PRINCIPLE**
>
> *Seeing It often has more to do with your ears than your eyes.*

lot of things that were my fault, things I had created of my own doing," Luis admits. "I had been gone a ton. I really hadn't done what I should have done to keep my marriage alive. I didn't put the effort into the home and kids that I should have." Despite his initial need to fight and be right, Luis had actually wronged himself and others. For all his desire to win, he had lost what was truly important to him.

Notice that no one outside of Luis changed. His wife didn't suddenly come to see the light. His boss didn't cut his hours. His kids didn't meet him in some alley and confess that they understood why he hadn't been around. Luis changed. Finding the courage, Luis chose to see things as they really were. Now he could move out of the victim cycle, stop living Below The Line, and take accountability to make life better for everyone.

The "See It" Question

Recognizing the need to See It is one thing. Actually Seeing It is another, because people want what they want and want it now. This wanting can be blinding.

"Melanie" was in love with a man she wanted to marry. Her parents and most of her friends warned her against marrying the guy—they could see he was nothing but trouble. But love is blind and, ignoring all advice, Melanie took the plunge. Fifteen hard years, three children, two bankruptcies, a series of her husband's indiscretions, and a lot of fighting later, it all ended with a bitter divorce. Only then could Melanie see what everyone else had known all along. What could have saved her all the heartache? What is the key to moving from Below The Line to Above The Line? Surprisingly, asking and answering one simple question:

What is the reality I most need to acknowledge?

Over the many years we've spent working with people who are trying to master the See It step, we've discovered that the very best way to overcome the blind spots and get a good view of reality is through feedback—important input about what you do well and how you can do even better, gained primarily in conversations with people who can help you see the whole picture. In fact, we've learned that the most accountable people seek feedback and that the ability to See It is directly related to the ability to get feedback. The two go hand in hand.

If you are a husband and want to know how you are doing in your marriage, ask your wife. Then ask your children—you may be surprised at what they've been just bursting to tell you. If you want to know how things are going at work, ask your boss and coworkers. How's it going at school? Ask your teachers and other students. How's it going on your team, whether it's a competitive sports team or a charity or volunteer group? Ask your teammates.

The best way to get feedback is to ask for it. It's not really more complicated than that. Simply ask: "What feedback do you have for me?" You can tailor your question to the situation; for example, "What feedback do you have for me on how I can be a better _____ (husband, wife, partner, friend, team member, employee, etc.)?"

Oz Principle

Accountable people seek feedback.

For this to work you will need to convince the person you are asking that you really do want to know what they think. Almost everyone worries about offering feedback, thinking it will backfire on them. They need to know they won't suffer any blowback from you if they honestly tell you how they see it.

After asking for the feedback, you then need to do the hard part and actually listen to what they're saying, no matter how painful. You will likely hear both appreciative feedback (what you do well) and constructive feedback (how you can improve). In either case, thank the person for whatever it is they told you. Gratitude will signal that you are not defensive (even if you are) and that you are happy they took the time to share.

Below are nine useful guidelines that can help you solicit, respond to, and use feedback to build your personal accountability:

Nine Guidelines for Getting and Using Feedback

1. Feedback doesn't just happen. You have to make it happen.

2. Seeking constructive feedback can be scary. Remind yourself that whomever you're asking feedback from is already thinking about you a certain way anyway; you're just hearing what they already believe.

3. It's easier for people to offer positive rather than negative observations. You have to ask for constructive feedback. Try "What can I do better?" instead of "What am I doing wrong?"

4. Most people believe others want positive rather than constructive feedback, so you might have

to convince them you really want to know what they think by just telling them that you value their honesty and opinion—no matter what it is.

5. Do not let constructive feedback, no matter how unpleasant, color your view of the person who's trying to help. Express sincere gratitude for their willingness to offer feedback in the first place.

6. Make getting feedback a habit, not a one-time thing.

7. Seek feedback even when you believe things are going great. This helps you to stay Above The Line.

8. After getting feedback, ask if it's okay to follow up with the person down the road; even suggest meeting again for a reality check just to keep yourself in line.

9. Finally, be nice to yourself. You can't make any important changes overnight.

Humility, gratitude, openness, honesty, patience with self, and a desire for better results are your best friends when it comes to getting feedback. Remember Jessie, our thirteen-year-old soccer player from chapter 3, who sat blindly on the bench until she asked her coach for feedback? Luis and Melanie would have given anything to understand this and seek feedback before their respective marriages were over. Feedback is key to overcoming blind spots and taking the all-important See It step to greater accountability and better results.

Oz Principle

Feedback creates accountable people.

What Happens When You Don't See It

You may remember the name Aron Ralston. He was the outdoor adventure seeker who ended up with his arm pinned by a boulder while hiking in southern Utah. Aron provides a compelling example of the painful consequences of not Seeing It, and also the saving power of finally opening your eyes to what you need to do.

When Aron parked his car and went for a hike in the Utah desert, he was blind to the danger. If he could have somehow looked at himself through the lens of a high-flying drone, he would have turned around. He would have seen the potential danger of a solo hike and wouldn't have so casually traipsed off without telling anyone where he was going—and without ample water or proper survival gear. He was an experienced outdoorsman and knew better, so why didn't he *see* any of this? Back to selective perception: He saw only what he wanted to see in order to justify doing what he wanted to do. Blind spots!

As Aron found out, not seeing can get anyone, no matter how smart or well trained, stuck "between a rock and a hard place." What started out as a half-day hike into Utah's red-rock country turned into a horrifying five-day nightmare. As Ralston recalls, "I dislodge . . . a large, 800-pound rock loose, that falls with me and eventually traps my right hand against the canyon wall." For days his desperate screams echoed off the sixty-foot sheer canyon of the narrows, but no one showed up to save him. No wizard. No good witch Glinda. Aron was stuck and alone and in real danger.

Acknowledging the reality—that no help was on the way—Aron made the decision to do the unthinkable: amputate his own right arm below the elbow with a pocketknife. This act not only saved him but also set him on a radically different path in other areas of his life. He's written a book, been the subject of a major film, gotten married, and become a father, and he now travels the world as a much-sought-after motivational speaker.

The ability to muster the courage to See It and examine your blind spots will not only help you avoid life's big problems but also help you with the little everyday troubles. The See It step is the first step Above The Line, and it must be taken with courage, resolve, and determination in order to grasp the full reality of what you are facing.

The View Is Great from Here!

Brian Regan is a popular stand-up comic, well known for his tales of woe about visiting the eye doctor. At one point he had not gone to the doctor to get his contact lens prescription updated for six years. He says, referring to the difference in clarity an updated eye prescription makes, if "you ever wait that long, then you get new lenses and you're like, man, I could have been *seeing* things!"

Now that you understand how and why to See It, you can be *seeing things*—and we hope you don't wait six years. Really seeing today means better results tomorrow.

If the Cowardly Lion chose to summon his courage and leave the shadows and seclusion of the forest to march up the yellow brick road, so can you. We promise you, the view is much better up Above The Line, where life is a lot more fun and rewarding for those whose eyes are wide open.

APPLY THE WISDOM: SEE IT!

Now we'd like you to apply the See It question specifically to that thing you said you really wanted back in chapter 1. Ask yourself:

What is the reality I most need to acknowledge in order to achieve the results I want in my life?

Now ask for feedback from people who are close to you. Ask them to answer that question honestly—convince them you want that feedback. Use that information to help you build a plan to achieve your goal or aspiration.

The
WISDOM
of
O'Z

Only by working up the courage to See It can you rise
above Below The Line excuses and achieve
your desired Above The Line results.

CHAPTER 5

The Tin Man: Finding the Heart to Own It

Tin Man: *Bang on my chest. . . . Go ahead—bang on it.*

Dorothy raps on his chest.

Scarecrow: *Beautiful! What an echo!*

Tin Man: *It's empty. The tinsmith forgot to give me a heart.*

Dorothy and Scarecrow: *No heart?*

Tin Man: *No heart . . . all hollow.*

Notice how the Tin Man blames his heartless predicament on his creator, claiming to be hollow inside because the tinsmith "forgot" to give him a heart. Did the tinsmith really forget, or did he just figure it was the Tin Man's job to develop heart himself?

As with everything related to accountability, true ownership does not come from outside—it comes from within. No one can make you Own It. There is no magic wand. That's why the Wizard was powerless to help Dorothy and her friends. Though they could rely on one another to some degree, ultimately they each had to follow their own passions, find their own heart, develop their own inner power to get what they wanted. It's no different for each of us.

Doina Oncel emigrated from Romania to Canada at seventeen. She eventually met an amazing guy, got married, started a business, and had two children. Things were going great until her husband started drinking. The drinking soon led to domestic abuse, the collapse of their business, and the loss of her marriage. A single mom and penniless, Doina saw her life spiral out of control until she found herself living with her children in a shelter. She had fallen about as Below The Line as someone could go. Then, after months in the shelter, her daughter said something that would change Doina's life: "Mommy, when I grow up I want to be just like you. You are the best mommy ever!"

Although she knew she *wasn't* the best mommy ever at the time, her daughter's words hit her hard, inspiring Doina to find the heart to take the Own It step and get a job and a better place to live—in short, to become the kind of person and the kind of mother her young daughter already believed she was.

Doina not only found work and a new home but also paid her bills and started taking classes and going to seminars. In the classes and seminars she used the grit and determination acquired from her past struggles to speak out, something that got her noticed by Bonnie Chan, leader of the Toronto chapter of Entrepreneurial Moms.

After Doina was recruited to work for the organization, she began devoting herself to encouraging other moms to take accountability for their lives. One success led to another, and Doina ended up running her own thriving business helping technology companies market themselves through social media.

We can all learn an important lesson from Doina's story: When you find the heart to Own It, you can and will change your world.

What It Means to Own It

We will never forget one business trip we took to Hawaii. During a break in a training session, we decided to take a quick tour of the island, and at one point we saw a number of people happily driving cars over the rough lava beds. We joked that whoever was beating up those cars could hardly be the owners—those cars had to be rentals.

That gave us an idea. Back at our training session, we brought up those lava-bed drivers as a way of introducing ownership, or in this case the lack of ownership. The examples caused a lot of embarrassed laughter when we discovered that those abused cars were indeed rentals—and the drivers were sitting right there in our own classroom!

Why do we care more for the things we "own" than for the things we "rent"? Perhaps it's because we don't have as much invested when we simply rent or borrow; there's not as much at stake. When you own something—whether it's a car, a work assignment, or a relationship—you make an investment, usually involving some degree of sacrifice. When you rent, you can walk away without losing anything. At the core of it, owners are just more invested than renters; they are "all in."

When it comes to achieving the result you want—that goal or objective that will make your life better—are you a renter or an owner? Are you approaching what you want with the high level of commitment, interest, and investment that only an owner can possess? Or are you going through the motions, only half committing to the goal, leaving yourself an easy exit in case things don't go the way you hoped?

> **OZ PRINCIPLE**
>
> *Ask yourself, are you a "renter" or an "owner"?*

A buddy in the Marines had an interesting story about his boot camp experience and what Owning It looked like to him. He said that they regularly held hand grenade–throwing competitions throughout camp. The competitions involved throwing a dummy grenade as far as you could, then running the other way. Drill instructors would then measure the distance between the two points. On the last day of boot camp, they would run this competition again—but using live ammo, real grenades! Not surprisingly, in this final test the distance between where the grenade hit and where the Marine ended up almost doubled over the previous ones. When you are "all in" and take ownership—whether you're running for your life or not—you will be motivated to do what you might otherwise never be able to.

This is what it means to take the Own It step Above The Line. It's the ability to dig deeper, to work harder, to stay at it longer—to feel and act like everything is on the line, that it's all up to you. It means maintaining a consistent "the buck stops here" mentality about what you do. This famous saying, popularized by U.S. president Harry Truman, is said to have originated from the game of poker. Back in the frontier days, a knife with a buckhorn handle was placed in front of the person who would

> **OZ PRINCIPLE**
>
> *To Own It means to leave it better than you found it.*

be dealing next. Players who did not want to deal could "pass the buck" to the next player until someone agreed to do it. "Passing the buck" became a slang expression for ducking accountability. True owners never duck; they have a vested interest in ensuring that the right things happen no matter what.

When you Own It, you take a "leave it better than you found it" approach to everything you do. You leave your fingerprints everywhere. People can see evidence that you were involved, that you left your own unique touch on what you were doing. That you made things better for having been there.

Owning It on the Job

We would go so far as to say that the ability to Own It is a key characteristic that often separates people who are highly successful from those who aren't. One popular business writer, Jeff Haden, describes the beliefs that remarkably successful people hold in common. One of those beliefs is the willingness to go the extra mile. But very few people actually go there. In fact, Haden states: "the extra mile is a vast, unpopulated wasteland." He explains, "Everyone says they go the extra mile. Almost no one actually does. Most people who go there think, 'Wait . . . no one else is here . . . why am I doing this?' and leave, never to return. That's why the extra mile is such a lonely place. That's also why the extra mile is a place filled with opportunities. Every time you do something, think of one extra mile thing you can do—especially if other people aren't doing that one thing. Sure, it's hard. But that's what will make you different. And over time, that's what will make you incredibly successful." When you Own It, you set yourself apart from the crowd.

Gallup, the polling group, has led an ongoing study of employee engagement in the workplace, examining people who are fully involved and enthusiastic about their jobs—in other words, people who Own It. Gallup's "State of the American Workplace Report" took a look at people from across different segments of the U.S. working population. Examining more than twenty-five million responses the researchers found that seven out of ten working Americans are "not engaged" or are "actively disengaged" in their work. That means seven out of every ten people celebrating at last year's office Christmas party didn't really want to be there. Seven out of ten in that meeting yesterday would have rather been bowling. So of the hundred million people in America who hold full-time jobs, only 30 percent are even remotely lit up by what they are doing at work.

Almost all current studies like this show that a sense of ownership and engagement is declining in the workplace, and some have even characterized much of the American workforce as "sleepwalking" through their jobs—staying busy but not making any real difference.

Both of the authors saw this firsthand early in our lives. One of us, at age sixteen, worked in the kitchen of a small restaurant and was flat-out told by his supervisor to "make a lot of noise; that way the owners will think we're working hard." He thought the guy was kidding until a few minutes later when he started banging pots together and throwing things around for no other purpose than to sound like he was working hard.

The other author remembers a summer job at a garden center in a senior living community. His work was to support his manager in making sure the residents had what they needed to plant their flower and vegetable gardens. Since it was summer in California, the heat could get pretty intense. He will never forget the day he sat in a cramped little shed with this manager and asked about the day's plan. The manager just said, "To sit. We are just going to sit in here all day. It's way too hot to work."

Sit? All day? After about five minutes he told the manager, "You may want to sit, but I'm here to work." The manager fired back, "If you go out and work, you'll make me look bad." The author went off to work. It was hot, but he was happy because he was there to work and do his job. It was an early experience that showed what not Owning It, what not being engaged looked like. It was a helpful illustration because, at that moment, he told himself that going through the motions would never be him.

We want you to stand out in your job, whether you're a musician, CEO, landscaper, supervisor, table setter, athlete, musician, cashier, artist, or forklift driver. Go that extra mile and Own It. You will enjoy what you do a lot more and work with a lot more enthusiasm. You will also be much more likely to get promoted, and make more money!

Tomorrow, when you go to work or school or do whatever it is you do, ask yourself whether you are truly owning what you're doing or just renting. Are you engaged or disengaged? Are you just "punching the clock" and blindly putting in your time, or are you inventive, creative, present, and fully there? Taking ownership will immediately separate you from the pack.

> ## Oz Principle
> *Go the extra mile; it will make you stand out from the crowd.*

The "Own It" Question

The question you should ask yourself to make sure you Own It is:

**How am I contributing to the problem
and/or solution?**

An honest answer to this question will inspire the kind of thinking that will help you find the path forward. If it's a problem you're trying to solve, your ability to Own It will pave the way for the next step Above The Line. If it is a challenge you are taking on, some goal or aspiration, some important result you're trying to make happen in your life—then an Own It mentality will fill you with the drive to get there.

The real power of this question lies in its focus on you. It's the "I" in the sentence that matters. *How am I contributing to the problem and/or solution?*

There are always factors outside your control that you cannot do anything about, so your focus has to be on what you *can* do, what you *can* control. When you focus on that, you set yourself up to find solutions. You free your ability to think creatively about your situation.

One busy father we know was overwhelmed with his job, the requirements at home, and the needs of others he was involved with in his volunteer work. He constantly felt anxious, depressed, and overloaded. He had gone way beyond that positive stress that motivates us to perform at our peak and was about to snap.

Then, one restless night while lying in bed thinking, the idea came to him to write down all the things he was worried about that he couldn't control. On a sheet of paper he made two columns. In the first one he listed all those things outside his control; in the second, all the things he could control and directly impact. It turned out to be a great exercise, as he realized that the things he could not control were things he should flat-out stop worrying about. He told himself to just forget them, not to focus on them or think about them, to get them out of his head. The column he could control would now receive his full attention and effort. What a change! Completely transformative.

This little Own It question exercise lifted his burden of worry and helped him see a way forward. He eventually conquered those challenges he could control and is today at the top of his field.

Making the Link

Taking the Own It step means being able to link where you are now with what you have done in the past and link where you want to be in the future with what you are going to do to get there. If you cannot make these links, then you don't Own It. In fact, you can't Own It. Making your desired results a reality requires you to own both the problem and the solution.

You may recall the old adage "If you are not part of the solution, you are part of the problem." Well, true ownership requires that you flip that: If you are not part of the problem, then you can't be part of the solution. This means much more than just admitting you're wrong. You have to be able to see your role in why things are the way they are. Though it might not seem like it, this is an empowering place to be, because owning the problem and how you contributed to it puts the solution within your reach. It makes the problem easier to conquer.

It will be a rare circumstance where you don't have at least some responsibility for your current situation. It can happen, of course. If a plane dropped out of the sky and landed on your car as you were driving to the grocery store, there's probably not a lot you could have done to prevent it. Sure, an extremist might suggest you somehow attracted it and should be held accountable for being in that spot at that time—but that's just crazy thinking!

When you are Below The Line and in the victim cycle, there is usually a "victim story" that explains why you're there. It's that story you've probably told a hundred times as a way of expressing your frustration—why you failed to do what you wanted to do. This story always includes all the reasons why it's not your fault and why life is just so unfair.

> ## Oz Principle
> *If you are not part of the problem, you can't be part of the solution.*

When we tell our victim stories, we often get a strong dose of sympathy from our audience as they relate their own situation to our woe-is-me tale. Take a moment and think of your own victim story—a time where you felt taken advantage of or victimized in some way. This doesn't need to be some big-deal story. In fact, most times it's not. It's usually something quite simple and related to everyday life.

The old cliché "There are two sides to every story" is generally true. The *victim side* stresses the part of the story that says you played no role in what happened. "The teacher doesn't like me, so, oh well, why try?" People most often fail to own their circumstances because they cannot bring themselves to accept the other side of the story— what we call the *accountable side*. When you focus only on what happens to you, as opposed to what you did or didn't do, you block out this other side of the story, the side that suggests you just might have played some part in it.

To Own It you must find the heart to see *both* sides of the story, linking what you have done, or failed to do, with your current circumstances. Seeing and owning the accountable side of your story does not mean suppressing or ignoring any facts that prove you have been victimized; it just means seeing the whole story, seeing both sides fairly, even the side that may bruise your ego a bit.

Here are some questions you can ask yourself to reveal the other, more accountable side of the story:

- What facts did you choose to ignore?
- What were the warning signs along the way?

- What would you advise someone who is facing the same situation?
- Given what you now know, what could you do differently to get a better result?

When you retell your story from the accountable point of view, it's like putting on a set of HD sunglasses—everything becomes so much clearer. Seeing things from this point of view puts you in a position to learn from the experience, so you can avoid making the same mistakes in the future. It also allows you to shed some baggage and emotionally get past the experience. By taking the accountable perspective, you empower yourself and increase the odds of success a hundredfold.

> **Oz Principle**
>
> *If you can't make the link, you don't Own It.*

Empower Yourself and Own It!

In an article entitled "Are We Happier?" that appeared in the *Los Angeles Times*, writer Leslie Dreyfous points out that though "the number of books on the topic [of happiness] has quadrupled in recent years and the therapy industry has more than tripled in size . . . baby boomers are four times likelier to say they're not satisfied with their lives than are people of their parents' generation . . . [and] the incidence of . . . depression is 10 times what it was pre–World War II."

We believe this spiraling lack of happiness today is simply due to a lack of accountability. Too often people blame their unhappiness on tough circumstances that they believe are beyond their control. They view painful situations as accidents, bad luck, or something that was done *to* them. But many of the problems we face in life are not accidents. Most of the time our problems are ones we bring on ourselves. This is why learning to Own It is so important.

The reality is, you pay a price when you don't Own It. You empower yourself when you do. The act of taking the Own It step is the act of giving yourself a sense of power—not power over someone else but power in and over yourself.

Making all the right connections in the Own It step sets you firmly on your own path of living in a world Above The Line—a world where frustration turns to focus, confusion turns to clarity, and pain turns to progress.

APPLY THE WISDOM: OWN IT!

Let's apply the Own It step to that goal you are trying to achieve or that problem you need to solve. Repeatedly ask:

How am I contributing to the problem and/or solution?

Look for ways to be an owner and not a renter. Consciously go the extra mile in life. Stand out. Be engaged. Recognize that there are two sides to every story.

The
WISDOM
of
OZ

The power already lies within you to overcome obstacles and get the result you want. You empower yourself when you take the Own It step.

CHAPTER 6

The Scarecrow:
Obtaining the Wisdom
to Solve It

Scarecrow: *Where's Kansas?*

Dorothy: *That's where I live. And I want to get back there so badly, I'm going all the way to Emerald City to get the Wizard of Oz to help me.*

Scarecrow: *Do you think if I went with you, this Wizard would give me some brains?*

Dorothy: *I couldn't say. But even if he didn't, you'd be no worse off than you are now.*

We all know what eventually happens to the Wizard of Oz: Dorothy's little dog, Toto, pulls back the curtain and reveals him to be a cheap circus magician from Nebraska. After meeting the wizard, it doesn't take Dorothy and her friends long to realize he can't help them. They come to learn what you already know: Solving It is about *you* creating *your* own way to move forward, *your* own way to overcome the obstacles *you* face in order to get what *you* want in life.

Typically, someone makes it to the Solve It step because they sincerely want to achieve some challenging goal or solve a sticky problem. Having a little faith that most problems can be solved is crucial to your ability to take this step Above The Line. This takes belief. It takes tenacity. It typically takes some real stick-to-itiveness to get where you want to go. The great news is that by following our Steps To Accountability, you will get there.

One example of belief, tenacity, and stick-to-itiveness is South African leader Nelson Mandela. You can only imagine that a man imprisoned for twenty-seven years might have thought his life was over, his goal of an apartheid-free South Africa hopeless. What would you be thinking after being unfairly locked up for so many years? Would you still have any kind of passion, desire, or goal? Any plans left? Could you even imagine that one day you would become the president of the very country that imprisoned you? Nelson Mandela could imagine it, which is why he got there.

Once he was released from prison, Mandela drew on all those years to become a voice of equality, helping overturn racial apartheid. Though a controversial figure much of his life, Mandela gained international praise for his humanitarian activism, receiving over 250 international honors, including the Nobel Peace Prize. Many in South Africa still refer to him as "Father of the Nation."

Today we live in a quick-fix world and get frustrated when our problems don't magically evaporate overnight. Solve It thinking suggests that you persist even when a quick fix doesn't happen, especially given that the quick fix most often isn't the best solution anyway.

Not long ago, one of the authors began the renovation of a new home. He soon found out the hard way that the garage doors didn't open quite as fast as those in his previous house. The author in question—who shall remain nameless to protect his pride—tells the story: "One day I was blindly 'text walking' through the garage when I slammed my head into the bottom of the rising garage door. I had fully expected it to be up by the time I got there. It just about knocked me over. I rubbed my head, only to find my hand covered in blood.

"At the doctor's office, the physician's assistant gave me a choice between glue or stitches. I asked which would do the best job of minimizing the scar. It was obvious that this guy wanted to glue it, because that was the quickest and most painless way to go—for him. But I wasn't after quick and painless, for him or me. I wanted the best long-term fix—after all, this is my face we were talking about. After some convincing, the PA finally admitted,

'We should probably stitch it.' So he stuck a needle in my head, numbed me up, and put in six stitches. Not fun, and admittedly more painful and difficult, but it did get the best result—you can hardly see a scar today. The other way, the quick-fix way, would have left a real mark on what my wife considers to be a very handsome head!"

When you take the Solve It step, prepare to go the distance. What you're after is likely not

> **OZ PRINCIPLE**
> *Look beyond the "quick fix."*

going to be easy. Most worthwhile pursuits aren't. Problems that seem to go on forever require determination to solve. When you're pursuing a major goal, it takes resolve, persistence, and a huge amount of passion to find solutions to overcome obstacles and make it happen.

What Solving It Looks Like

The Solve It state of mind is a creative, "as if my life depended upon it" kind of thinking, thinking that brings solutions for challenges and obstacles that we often believe are outside our control. If your life depended on it, would you come up with any new ideas, new approaches, or new thinking that would allow you to make progress and move forward? If the answer is actually no, then you've probably done all you can do.

It was three thirty in the morning when John Aldridge, a New York fisherman, fell from his moving lobster boat forty miles off the shore of Long Island. Nobody survives the cold Atlantic for long, so after his initial futile screams for help, and treading water in a panic, John faced a choice: prepare to drown or start thinking.

The first thing any experienced fisherman knows to do if he ends up overboard is to get rid of his boots; boots are dead weight that will drag you down. But John's urgent Solve It thinking led him to a very creative, even life-saving solution. He took off one boot, flipped it upside down, and, between rising swells, lifted the boot over his sinking head and pulled it down hard into the water, trapping air. Then, sticking that boot under his arm to help keep him floating, he did the same thing with his other boot. Now instead of dead weights, his two boots were life-saving floats. Genius!

But what now? John knew that his boots couldn't keep him floating forever. That took too much effort. He was still bobbing forty miles off the coast, completely alone, in the dark, with three long hours to wait until daylight—three hours before his fishing partner, sleeping belowdecks, would even know he was missing and call the Coast Guard for help.

Most of us picture the Atlantic as just a rolling, flat mass of water. But Aldridge had fished this area for twenty years and knew where he was. He also knew other lobster fishermen had dropped traps along the ocean floor nearby. You can spot these traps because lobstermen tie a brightly colored buoy to each end of the trap lines. If John could reach one of these buoys, he could hang on and be more visible for anyone looking for him.

It was two hours after sunrise when Aldridge crested a wave and spotted a buoy a few hundred yards away. Tired, thirsty, and weak, he wasn't sure he could make it, so he took off a sock and stuck it over a hand to help him swim—another bright Solve It idea. He made it to the buoy, cut it free, and eventually made it to a second buoy, tying the two together with a few feet of buoy rope to form a sort of raft.

After his fishing partner realized he was missing and called for help, twenty-one boats, several helicopters, and a host of Coast Guard personnel searched over six hundred square miles of open ocean for John. Finally, an excited voice crackled over the

Oz Principle

Think as if your life depended on it.

radios: "We have your man. He's alive." John Aldridge had been floating in the Atlantic for twelve hours.

As John Aldridge can attest, a Solve It mentality can create a survive-it solution in even the most dire of times. Now your situation—that goal you want to achieve or the problem you need to solve—won't likely be a life-or-death scenario, but creative solutions come when you put everything on the line. So when you take the Solve It step, think as if your life depended on it. While your life may not be at risk, your happiness is.

The "Solve It" Question

When taking the Solve It step, you should ask:

What else can I do?

Asking this over and over is the key to making progress. Repeatedly asking, *What else can I do?* forces you to drill down through any obstacles to find solutions, solutions that are often buried deep in the rich soil of innovation and creativity, solutions that almost always lurk below the surface of your easygoing, everyday, even routine way of thinking.

Finding solutions is just like digging for gold. We've become fans of the Discovery Channel reality TV show *Gold Rush*, one of the most-watched Friday-night programs of all time. The show follows the lives of a few groups of modern-day miners as they compete against time, one another, and nature in hopes of striking it rich. Their bottom-line secret to success: Move a lot of dirt.

It's quite a process. First the miners must remove a top layer, called the overburden. This can mean moving six to twelve feet of rock and dirt before any real mining even starts. Below this worthless and painful six to twelve feet, they hit the pay gravel or paydirt. The more paydirt the miners process, the more gold they potentially find. In the end they must move several tons of dirt to find just one ounce of gold. It's that simple—and that hard.

The Solve It lesson from gold mining is to work hard and be prepared to move a lot of dirt! Solutions may be hard to find at first, so keep trying. Don't give up. Keep asking, *What else can I do?*

Taking the Solve It step is not for the faint of heart. It is hard work, but will yield rich rewards. If you are willing

> **Oz Principle:**
> *You've got to move a lot of dirt to get the gold.*

to stay with it, you will eventually hit paydirt and find the nuggets of wisdom that will yield the solutions you are looking for.

There was once a fairly routine six-hundred-meter track race at the University of Minnesota. We wouldn't be talking about it now if Heather Dorniden hadn't fallen flat on her face during the race and turned the routine into the remarkable. What makes the race and Heather noteworthy is what she did *after* she landed flat on her stomach in the dirt. (The YouTube video is amazing!)

If a Below The Liner fell, she might lie there for a while feeling sorry for herself, blaming her shoes, the poor track, or the runner next to her before slinking off to the bleachers for a good cry. Not Heather. It's hard to believe how quickly she picked herself up. How fast she ran until she caught the other runners. How amazed the awestruck fans were. And how inspiring it was to see her win. Yes, we said "win."

Why was it instinct for Heather to bounce up so fast after she fell? It starts to make sense when you pull back the curtain on who she is as a person. At the time of the race, Heather was a senior majoring in kinesiology with a 3.9 GPA, scholarships, and an NCAA indoor championship in the eight hundred meters as a freshman. She was an eight-time All-American and the most decorated University of Minnesota woman track star ever. She popped back up and won the race because she had learned to Solve It a long time ago. She had made a habit of quickly asking her own version of *What else can I do?*

We want you to make it a habit too, because it's not normal to succeed every time. People fall down. Successful people don't always win, but they do spring back up when they fall. Your Solve It ideas won't always work. Solve It thinking means to keep trying, keep moving. Go at it again. Pick yourself up and keep running no matter what, every time. We like the way football coach Vince Lombardi put it: "The greatest accomplishment is not in never falling, but in rising again after you fall."

How to Solve It

Let's play a little game. You may have seen it before. It's called the nine dots puzzle, and it was developed in 1914 as an exercise to teach creative thinking. For something to stick around that long, it must be good, right?

Below you'll see a small matrix of nine dots. Your challenge is to try connect all of them with only four straight lines, never going through any dot twice and without lifting your pen or pencil from the page. Go ahead and give it a shot.

• • •

• • •

• • •

Were you able to Solve It? In our expeerience, 90 percent of you trying it for the first time won't be able to figure it out. Of those of you who have seen it before but have forgotten, only about one in four will remember and be able to solve it again. In other words, this seemingly simple puzzle is not so simple. You can see the solution at the end of the chapter, but before you go there keep in mind that the point of the exercise is not finding the right solution but *thinking differently about how to solve the problem.*

Did you draw an imaginary square box connecting all the outside dots and think you had to stay inside that? We naturally tend to place boundaries on our thinking, so we often do it even when no one tells us to. Putting this mental box around the dots is what most people do, and it's that self-imposed wall around the problem that makes it impossible to solve. The only way to Solve It is to *think outside the box.*

There are also other mistakes people commonly make, like not drawing anything at all. They just stare at the dots as if willing them to yell out an answer! The best way to Solve It, of course, is to try drawing it over and over. *Action often produces results, even if we don't know what we are doing.* Remember our writer friend's quote from chapter 3, "Do *something*, even if it's wrong"? Often in our quest to be perfect and not to look the fool, we do nothing and become a fool anyway.

Here are some suggestions about how to think outside the box, suggestions that will help you deal creatively with any obstacles you meet during the Solve It step. When reading these, consider that goal you want to achieve or that problem you are trying to solve.

Brainstorm with the Right People

Tough problems require new ideas; brainstorm with someone who can help you. Try to find someone who has achieved a similar goal or solved a similar problem. When brainstorming, don't label any ideas as stupid, at least not yet. Loosen up your thinking. Write ideas down. The longer the list, the better. Wait for an idea you really feel great about.

Keep Asking, What Else Can I Do?

Ask this question repeatedly over several days. Allow your mind time to think about it. Don't just force an answer in one sitting. This process encourages you to study problems with fresh thinking that will inspire better options.

Think Differently
(as we stressed in Chapter 2)

One way to do this is to interview other people and ask, "What would you do?" Describe the situation. Don't tell them what you have thought of; just let them give you their unbiased view on how they would approach it. And take a lot of notes!

Do Your Homework

A new approach requires new information. Hello, library. Hello, Internet. There are over seven billion people on the planet and a World Wide Web filled with ideas. You are probably not the first one trying to overcome this obstacle or solve this problem. Find out what others did and how it worked for them.

Test Your Assumptions

Most of us limit ourselves with imagined boundaries that may not really exist, but because we fail to test them they define our reality. Test your assumptions, those ideas you think could work. Ask how you can get outside the box. Fight for new ways of thinking.

> ### OZ PRINCIPLE
> *Action often produces results, even if you don't know what you are doing.*

Having a Solve It mentality means developing and honing a creative mind-set. It's about pushing yourself to think differently, to try new ideas and see if they work.

How Great Solving It Can Be!

We've been sharing some pretty hair-raising, life-and-death stories that may grab headlines or make for good movies, but most of us never face such perils as bobbing in the chilly Atlantic or spending twenty-seven years in a

South African prison. So just how does the Solve It step work for the everyday you?

Larry Swilling's wife was in desperate need of a kidney transplant. Most people would just stick their name on a list, then sit back and hope for a new kidney to show up. But not seventy-eight-year-old Larry Swilling, who had devoted himself to his wife for fifty-five years. Knowing his wife's name appeared far down the list and seeing how rapidly her health was failing, Larry faced a choice: watch her "drown in the Atlantic" or help her "swim to safety." He got Above The Line by essentially asking himself, *What else can I do to help find my wife a kidney?* And he did something to Solve It.

Donning a sandwich board proclaiming, NEED KIDNEY 4 WIFE, he started walking around his hometown of Anderson, South Carolina: day after day, week after week, month after month. According to CBS News, after a year and more than 250 walking miles, Larry had found thousands of people willing to offer their kidneys. More than a hundred actually underwent the necessary testing. In the end, retired navy lieutenant commander Kelly Weaverling, forty-one, was found to be the perfect match to save Jimmy Sue Swilling's life.

Following his wife's successful life-saving surgery, Larry Swilling bear-hugged the doctors and thanked Lieutenant Weaverling for her sacrifice. Jimmy Sue said,

"I knew it was going to happen. . . . Larry would not have stopped."

A donated kidney, a saved wife, a heroic organ donor, and thousands moved to action—all because one humble guy was willing to get Above The Line.

APPLY THE WISDOM: SOLVE IT!

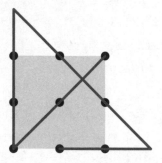

The answer to the nine dots puzzle brilliantly illustrates how many solutions do, in fact, lie *outside the box*, outside the lines, outside your normal, habitual way of thinking. Now put "What else can I do?" to work on your desired goal or stubborn problem. Ask it over and over. Put a list of possible solutions on paper. If you're still struggling, brainstorm, think differently, do your homework, and test your assumptions.

Every successful journey Above The Line begins
by asking a single question: What else can I
do to achieve the result I want?

CHAPTER 7

Dorothy:
Exercising the Means
to Do It

Glinda: *Are you ready now? . . . Then close your eyes and tap your heels together three times and think to yourself, There's no place like home, there's no place like home . . .*

Dorothy: *There's no place like home . . . There's no place like home . . .*

A s you may recall, in *The Wizard of Oz* Dorothy eventually discovered that all she had to do was click her heels three times and focus on what she most wanted by saying: "There's no place like home." From the moment she touched down in Oz, her ability to exercise the means to Do It and enlist the help of her friends, listen to the advice of those she trusts, show resourcefulness in solving her problems, and being patient with staying the course so that she could make it back home—all moved her beyond angry apple trees, poisoned poppies, flying monkeys, and wicked witches. She knew what she wanted to accomplish and kept after it.

Exercising the means to Do It involves more than just trying harder. When we take the Do It step, we move beyond trying to doing. We've always liked the exchange between Luke and Yoda in the movie *Star Wars Episode V: The Empire Strikes Back*. Yoda, frustrated with Luke's doubt, says: "Always with you it cannot be done. Hear you nothing that I say? You must unlearn what you have learned." Luke responds, "Alright, I'll give it a try." Oops! Wrong answer, Luke! Yoda, a little irritated with his new pupil: "No! Try not. Do or do not. There is no try."

Yoda was right when it comes to the Do It step and achieving what you want: Trying is just not in the equation. It's all about doing.

What Do You Really Want?

Both of the authors have volunteered time to work with thousands of teens over the years. One had a simple question he would often ask these young people: "What do you want?" While they shouted out their wish lists, the author would scribble them down the left side of a chalkboard as fast as he could: a new car, a new phone, a better boyfriend.

After filling the board he would stop and compliment them; they definitely knew what they wanted!

Then he would ask them a second question: "What do you really want?" The word "really" changed everything. They'd go quiet, thinking about what they *really* wanted. Suggestions would slowly start coming, things like happily married parents, a sibling not having cancer, or a friend getting off drugs. As the list built down the right side of the board, the feeling in the room would change from Christmas-morning exuberance to reflection and resolution.

Pulling back and looking at the board, he would then ask what the difference was between the two lists. The answers were always the same. Unlike the list on the left, those things listed down the right side of the board were worth fighting for; the teens would sacrifice, would work with everything in them to go after those things. Over the years, while the faces of the teens have changed, the results have always been the same: There is a difference between what we want and what we *really* want. Our commitment to get what we *really* want must include a "Do or do not; there is no try" kind of attitude and approach. That's the only way we will ever Do It!

For an inspiring example, consider Ben Carson, an inner-city Detroit native, son of a teen mother who married at thirteen and a runaway father. There was a time that Ben honestly believed he was "the dumbest kid in the fifth grade." But his mother, Sonya, rather than letting her son succumb to victim thinking, encouraged accountability. She tossed the TV from their tiny Detroit home and made him hit the library, where he was expected to read and write reports on two books a week.

At this point he was faced with a choice: Would he respond to his mother's mandate to spend extra time after school improving and preparing himself, or would he push back, rebel, and refuse to become a better student? Ben chose the former. He chose to learn, to improve, and to Do It. All that reading and writing improved his school grades, and he eventually worked his way from the bottom of his fifth-grade class to the top of one of the most challenging professions in the world as professor of neurosurgery, oncology, plastic surgery, and pediatrics at John Hopkins University. He was the first surgeon to suc-cessfully separate twins joined at the head. He's been awarded thirty-eight honorary doctorate degrees, dozens of national merit citations, and the Presidential Medal of Freedom, the nation's

> **OZ PRINCIPLE**
>
> *Nothing great happens until you do something.*

highest civilian honor. Even with all he has achieved, Dr. Carson has never forgotten where he came from, becoming an advocate of America's inner cities and an outspoken critic of entitlements and dependency. Sounds a lot like he lived Above The Line accountability, doesn't it? Ben Carson made this kind of life for himself by taking one Do It step after another while avoiding the ever-present pitfalls found on any journey Above The Line.

Walking in Circles

Have you ever felt that after setting off on a journey to accomplish your goal or to solve a pesky problem, you were wandering in endless circles, unable to make any real progress? Even when you're ready to Do It and focus on the direction you want to go, the littlest things can veer you quickly and surprisingly off course.

There's a scientific explanation for this mental merry-go-round. German scientists Jan Souman and Marc Ernst published a study in the journal *Current Biology* that looked at paths taken by people walking for several hours in the Sahara Desert and the Bienwald Forest—at locations and times purposely chosen to block out any orienting clues such as a mountain or the position of the sun. Using GPS to record their subjects' routes, the researchers discovered that, without any clues to help them stay on course or figure out where they were, people would naturally drift away from a straight line and end up, quite literally, walking in circles.

When you set off to Do It, how can you keep from walking in circles—that is, going through the motions but making no real progress? First, you must have a clear path.

It may not be a yellow-brick-road kind of clear, but you should lay out a clear plan with the steps you will take to accomplish whatever it is you want to accomplish. Second, you need determination to do the things you said you would do—the will to follow through on your plan, even in the face of obstacles, doubt, fear, or past failure. We have always liked the saying "Make your plan, then work your plan, then watch your plan work!"

One more caution: You must prepare to be tested in your resolve to succeed as you take the Do It step. Every good thing you want to accomplish—solving a problem or achieving a goal—comes with its own challenges, and you will certainly come across some of these on your journey:

⚠ Your faith in your ability to Do It will be tested.

⚠ Your desire to get it done will be challenged, your resolve stretched.

⚠ Your ability to stay Above The Line will be tried.

⚠ Your willpower to overcome obstacles will be drained by a desire to take the easy way out or slip back into the comfort of bad habits.

Here's what we have learned when it comes to these soul stretchers: *You've got to want it more than you don't want it.* Everything will exact a certain price from you—energy, effort, patience, resources, challenges . . . the list goes on. It's only natural to want to have the good things in life without paying the price. You want to lose weight but don't want to sacrifice your favorite food or sweat through all the exercise. You want to be a best-in-class athlete but don't want to endure the training required to get there. You want that promotion but don't want to put in the extra hours. Success only comes when you hit that tipping point and you want it *more* than you don't want it. That's when real movement occurs.

> ## Oz Principle
> *You've got to want it more than you don't want it.*

The "Do It" Question

There are a lot of quotes and mantras out there inspiring you to pay the "want it" price, from New England Patriots coach Bill Belichick's "Do your job" to Nike's famous "Just do it" to race car driver Mario Andretti's "Do it no matter what." All make the same bottom-line point: Nothing great happens until *you do* something. Only by *your doing* can *you* experience the soaring results that come from living Above The Line.

The following all-important Do It question should help you concentrate on what you need to do to get what you're after. At this stage of the Steps To Accountability, ask yourself:

What am I accountable to do and by when?

By asking this question you remove any potential for confusion and you create a concrete plan of action—a plan that includes all the things you are going to do and the dates and times by which you are going to do them. Be sure to break down your plan into small, achievable pieces. You can't eat an elephant in one bite. (In fact, it takes about 250 days to cat one elephant. That's 31,930 bites!)

The takeaway: If you're trying to achieve something big or difficult, pace yourself. But don't let that pace give you permission to lollygag; always include a "by when" date and time in your plan. You should feel accountable for your "by when" and do everything in your power to follow through by the time you set.

Finally, if you want to increase the probability of doing it, tell someone about it. Make your plans and deadlines visible; put yourself out there. There is power in sharing your plans, in transparency—power that will help you Do It!

The Gravitational Pull Below The Line

When you are working to Do It, there is a gravitational force constantly tugging on you, trying to drag you down Below The Line. Just as massive planets produce gravity, drawing everything toward them, it seems that tough problems and challenging obstacles have enough mass to pull you away from getting what you want. This force gets bigger and stronger as the challenges get larger and tougher.

These Below The Line forces possess power because they are legitimate issues, real reasons not to move forward. They're not made up. They are genuine and often seem beyond your control. It's easy to rattle off these roadblocks as reasons you are not making progress or moving forward. But those reasons become *excuses* as soon as you start using them to stop trying to solve the problem.

> **OZ PRINCIPLE**
> *Don't let gravity pull you down.*

Let's talk for a minute about two of those forces constantly tugging you Below The Line—those reasons that can so easily become excuses.

First: Other People. There is an often-told story of some behavioral scientists who conducted an experiment involving monkeys, stairs, and a few bananas. The scientists stuck five monkeys in a large roomlike cage, with bananas sitting at the top of a set of stairs. Before long, a monkey went up the stairs for the bananas, at which point the scientists soaked the other four innocent bystander monkeys with ice-cold water. Soon another monkey made the attempt and the process was repeated—the other monkeys were soaked with water. It didn't take long until every time a monkey went for the bananas, the other four would beat him before he got there—they did not want to get drenched again! Scientists soon discovered that the monkeys stopped going after the bananas for fear of getting pounded on by the group.

The scientists then decided to bring in a new monkey, one who had not yet been included in the experiment, swapping him for one of the originals. The first thing the new monkey did was head for the bananas. You can guess what happened: The other four went nuts and beat on the new guy. After a number of beatings, Mr. New Monkey said, *Forget this*, and stopped going for the bananas, even though he knew nothing about the ice water.

Then the researchers put in a second new monkey in place of one of the originals, and the same thing happened. The other four, including Mr. New Monkey, pounded on this second new guy until he got with the program. Then the scientists swapped in a third new monkey. Then a fourth. Finally all five monkeys had been subbed out, and the result was still the same: Any new monkey trying for the bananas would get a beating, even though by now not *one* of them had ever been doused with the ice water. None of them had any idea why they were beating on one another, no idea why going up the stairs to get bananas was a bad idea. It had just become the way things worked in this cage!

The point of the story? The people around us and the views they have been conditioned to hold can either help us or hurt us when it comes to "going for the bananas." Sometimes we can fail to Do It because *that's just the way things work in this cage!* Ask yourself: Are the people you spend time with good for you? Are you good for them? Are you beating up on one another with no idea why? Are you afraid to buck the system or ask why things are done the way they're done?

Second: Health. This will likely affect your ability to Do It at one time or another. According to one study, seven in ten people admit they frequently go to work sick. That's a big number. So if you've ever gone to work not feeling well and thinking you should have stayed home, maybe you can take solace in the fact that there's a whole lot of other people working right there alongside you who may not feel all that great either.

To say that one of the authors has experienced some significant health issues would be an understatement. What he went through would have made falling Below The Line easy for any of us. Here's his story.

"A wrestling match with my son resulted in a broken back. And though, yes, I pinned him, the real news during the visit to the doctor about my sore back was the discovery of stage 4 lymphoma. Cancer. It was all through my body; there was even a tumor the size of a Nerf football in my abdomen that I never knew about.

"Over the ensuing months, many amazing doctors, seven chemo treatments, four spinal taps, intense family support, and some significant divine intervention brought the good news: full remission. Then came the recovery from the recovery. The steroids used in treatment had triggered avascular necrosis (AVN), something casually referred to as 'bone death,' where bone cells die from poor blood supply to the joints. It took ten surgeries over five years to make the needed repairs—including full replacements of both hips and both shoulders.

"Here's what I learned: You have to decide if you are sick or healthy; you can't be both. When you're sick, you are on the bench. Out of the game. When you're healthy, you are on the field, out there in the middle of it all. I remember consciously asking myself, *What do you want, healthy or sick? You can't be both.*

"I made the choice to be healthy. That did not mean I could or even should ignore the problems or pretend they weren't there. Hardly. These were pretty intense issues to work through. What it did mean, though, was that I had to give up the sympathy that normally comes with being sick. You know, the 'Oh, wow, that must be so frustrating,' 'That's awful,' 'You must be in pain all the time,' 'It's really amazing that you can even do what you do,' 'I would have never guessed,' and 'You deserve some medal or something for even getting out of bed.'

"The downside of choosing healthy is you don't get any of that. You have to pretend you're feeling great even when you're not, or at least keep your problems to yourself so that you still look like a player. I have come to believe something that my friend, business partner, and coauthor of this book shared with me many years ago when we first wrote *The Oz Principle*, something he learned from one of his mentors: 'Most of the work in this world gets done by people who don't feel very well.' So I kept my health issues largely to myself and stayed in the game in my work and at home.

"Looking back, I was very fortunate that it wasn't worse. There are so many suffering people with stories far more compelling and miraculous. But the story is not the point; it's the lesson. In all the cases I know where people have endured horrible health challenges and carried on in spite of them, they all simply made the choice to be well."

Now, please don't misunderstand, we are not saying that everyone who is sick can or even should pretend they are well. Serious health issues strike people and can totally immobilize them. What we are saying is that the day-to-day health challenges that plague most of us come with a choice: let it pull you down or rise above it all.

> ## Oz Principle
>
> *Reasons become excuses as soon as you start using them to stop trying to solve the problem.*

Doing What You Say You Will Do

It's tempting to sum up Dorothy's journey by saying that she obviously just wanted it badly enough. But though there's no doubt she really wanted to get back to Kansas, getting home took more than desire. She needed to recognize and pay the price, using all of herself, all the skills she already possessed. She had a plan and knew what she and her new friends needed to do and when they needed to do it. This kind of focused action comes from committing yourself at whatever cost, discovering your own unique means for Doing It, and then Doing It until it's done. Imagine if Dorothy had stopped before bringing the witch's broom back to the Wizard. She had come so far, but all her effort would have meant nothing had she and her friends not finished the job.

Doing It is more than just working harder. It's more than just fighting like crazy against any obstacle. It's organizing what you're going to do. It's working smart. Building a plan, following a path, bringing a logical flow into your actions.

While Dorothy had worn the ruby slippers her entire journey, she could not tap their power until she had traveled a long, hard road of discovery. Only then could all her effort and experience combine to convince her that clicking her heels would really work. Only then could she return to Kansas.

APPLY THE WISDOM: DO IT!

Whether it's risk, fear, laziness, health difficulties, toxic associations, or any other inhibiting factor, there will most likely come a time when you hit the Do It wall. To keep yourself Above The Line and moving forward, make sure you repeatedly ask:

What am I accountable to do and by when?

Then make a plan with the steps you need to take—things that you can do that are within your control—and follow through to do what you say you will do.

The
WISDOM
of
OZ

Do It means wrapping your arms completely around
what you need to do and when you need to do it,
and then doing what you say you will do
to make it happen.

CHAPTER 8

You've Always Had the Power . . .

Dorothy: *Oh, will you help me? Can you help me?*

Glinda: *You don't need to be helped any longer. You've always had the power to go back to Kansas.*

Dorothy: *I have?*

Scarecrow: *Then why didn't you tell her before?*

Glinda: *Because she wouldn't have believed me. She had to learn it for herself.*

At the end of *The Wizard of Oz* we learn that Dorothy always had the power to go back to Kansas—she just didn't know it. Not even the good witch Glinda's magical power could whisk Dorothy home; she had to discover this power inside herself—the power to control her circumstances and not let her circumstances control her. The same applies to all of us. And when that discovery happens, the sky's the limit for what we can achieve.

Believe it or not, Walt Disney followed the same empowering path of internal discovery. Walt was fired from one of his first animation jobs, at the *Kansas City Star* newspaper, because the boss felt he "lacked imagination and had no good ideas." Disney then worked for the film studio Laugh-O-Gram, which soon went bankrupt because he and those with him couldn't manage money. A one-two punch like this would knock most people Below The Line and render hope unconscious. But Walt, with his brother Roy, moved to Hollywood, founded a studio, invented Mickey Mouse and Disneyland, won twenty-two Academy Awards (more than any other single person in history), and built what would become the Walt Disney Company—a worldwide business that today brings in around $45 billion a year while entertaining millions. Pretty good for a guy who "lacked imagination and had no good ideas."

Far from the glittery world of Hollywood was Stacy, a young girl in junior high school. She was grossly overweight, wracked by low self-esteem, and consumed by what others thought of her. Her parents had tried everything to get her to be more active and eat smarter. They went on family walks, encouraged her to be active, even built a swimming pool. Nothing worked. Why? Because no one else could lose weight for her. No one else could get her in shape. Not until Stacy made the *personal choice* to rise above her circumstances could anything change. Fortunately, Stacy finally did make that choice. She started eating smarter and exercising—and went on to lose seventy pounds! As a result, Stacy's self-esteem skyrocketed, and in just two short years she became president of her high school class. Today Stacy is a certified personal trainer who works out six days a week, has two beautiful children, prides herself on healthy cooking and eating, and recently ran her first marathon with her husband.

Oz Principle

Make it happen!

Despite their vastly different backgrounds and desires, Walt Disney and Stacy, and even fictional Dorothy, all did exactly the same thing: *made the personal choice to take control of their lives* and overcome all the traps, tricks, and troubles that we all face. The results of doing so can be miraculous—for your own life and the countless lives you go on to touch.

Unleash the Power!

Now that you've made it to our final chapter, you should have learned more about the power of personal accountability than you ever knew before, maybe even more than

you've ever wanted to know. We hope you are ready to unleash this very real power in your life.

Now, how do you do that? How do you really make
personal accountability work for you? Wouldn't it be easy
if there were just some switch you could flip? A button you
could push? Maybe an app you could use? Well, that magic
switch-flipping app button really does exist—it's called
making a choice and acting on it.

Your choices—*acts of selecting from two or more possi-
bilities*—will either move you Above The Line, where you
take charge of making it happen, fulfilling your aspira-
tions, or solving that problem you face, or drop you Below
The Line, where you risk wallowing in the blame game
while getting trapped in the victim cycle.

But you can't be in two places at one time. That may
seem obvious, but it is human nature to straddle the line,
to sit on the fence, to wait and see. "I want to lose weight,
but I wanna eat what I want." "I like the commitment and
security of married life, but I love the freedom of being
single." In the end, you have to choose one or the other.

We can take a page out of history from Alexander the
Great. While we are not big fans of his plan for world
domination, he did know how to keep his troops from being in two places at once. Facing a Persian army that
vastly outnumbered his own, upon landing on the Persian beach Alexander ordered his men to burn their own
boats. His troops now had no escape: The only way to re-

turn home would be in their enemy's boats. Alexander had their attention.

With respect to any given situation, you're either Above The Line or Below The Line. But you can't choose accountability and be Above The Line in a general way and yet reserve the right to be Below The Line with respect to certain problems, annoying relationships, or whiny complaints you may deal with every day. The only way to tap into the power of personal accountability is to adopt an Above The Line attitude and approach in *everything* you do.

We now invite you to make this powerful choice to live Above The Line and enjoy all the benefits that come with the accountable life. We're not just talking about a passive decision to do better. We're asking that you make a deep, abiding choice to live Above The Line. Starting today. Now. This minute.

> ## Oz Principle
>
> *You can't be in two places at one time—choose to be Above The Line.*

This kind of commitment does not come easily. You must dig for it, but once you feel it, you will find everything you do supercharged with new energy and focus because *you've* made that never-turn-back, burn-the-bridges decision to take personal accountability.

The Air Is Better Above The Line

It's really true: The world *is* better Above The Line. Just like a breath of fresh air, accountability allows a person to think more clearly about everything. Given our ongoing thirty-year experience studying the impact of personal accountability in people's lives, and with millions of people as our "laboratory," we have come to realize that accountable, Above The Line people enjoy quite a few benefits. They . . .

- are empowered to see things as they really are
- find solutions that most others don't
- learn and grow from negative experiences when others would get stuck
- avoid having problems in the first place
- enjoy better, stronger, more fulfilling relationships
- experience less of the stress and depression that always comes with victimization
- have more inner confidence that they can Do It
- laugh more
- earn more promotions
- make more money
- gain more respect
- smile more

- are happier
- are healthier
- appear smarter
- and . . . are better looking!

We may have gotten a little carried away with the last one here, but you get the point: Greater accountability brings all kinds of personal payoffs. Think about the accountable people you know, those who operate Above The Line; those who are regularly flipping the accountability switch and getting things done. Don't you find that the majority of these benefits are part of their lives?

We're not talking about the arrogance and conceitedness you find in someone who tends to get what they want no matter the consequences to other people. This kind of person isn't Above The Line; they can't be. Accountable people are not just accountable for making positive changes for themselves; they are also accountable for their relationships and the experiences they create for others. The positive benefits that come from being Above The Line are practically endless, provided you make the choice. Given what's on the above list, who wouldn't want a piece of that?

> **OZ PRINCIPLE**
>
> *The most important person to get Above The Line is you.*

Put It to the Test

While inaction is the assassin of accountability, taking the right actions will accelerate your journey to results. And those actions are the Steps To Accountability; to See It, Own It, Solve It, and Do It. This means asking yourself the right questions to help you achieve your goal, solve the problem, or finally experience the performance break-through you've been looking for.

Now it's time to put it to the test and experience for yourself the power of personal accountability by applying our four Above The Line questions to what you want. Remember, the trick is answering these questions as honestly and candidly as you can.

First, identify what you want:

What I want: _____

_____

_____

_____

Now apply the accountability questions we have presented throughout the book to what you want. You may decide to do this on your own or find someone you can brainstorm with. As you've learned, each of these questions is specifically designed to help you effectively move Above The Line.

1. See It: What Is the Reality I Most Need to Acknowledge?

This question is key to figuring out what is really going on. Here are other questions you can ask yourself to expand your ability to See It:

- What is not working?
- What are the "hard things" I need to hear?
- Who do I need to ask for feedback?
- What am I pretending not to know?

Your answers to these questions will help you see the whole picture. Once you do, pay attention to the reality you most need to acknowledge so you can make some real progress.

2. Own It: How Am I Contributing to the Problem and/or Solution?

The answer to this question will help you see why you are where you are and what you can do about it. Some additional questions you can ask yourself:

- What role have I played in my current circumstances?
- Am I trying to be in two places at one time?

- Am I totally committed to moving forward?
- What feedback would I give someone else in this same situation?

Your answers here will reveal opportunities for ownership and investing fully in making it happen.

3. Solve It: What Else Can I Do?

Your answers to the powerful Solve It question will reveal new ways to move forward and see real progress. Consider these additional questions:

- If everything depended upon me, what else would I do?
- What can I control that I have assumed is outside of my control?
- If I were to do things differently, what would I do?
- If my life depended upon it, what else would I do?

Solving It requires all of your creative instincts and can be assisted by seeking input from others to brainstorm solutions. Be careful not to spin your wheels on things you cannot control—focus on what you can control or influence.

4. Do It: What Am I Accountable to Do and by When?

This final Above The Line question will help you lock in a specific plan to move forward. Additional questions you can ask yourself:

- What realistic deadlines can I give myself?
- Have I broken down the plan into simple, actionable steps?
- Who can I tell my plan and report my progress to?
- What adjustments would make my plan even more realistic?

The key is to stay Above The Line as you put it all together and Do It. Don't be discouraged if it takes some time to make the progress you want to make. In his book *Outliers: The Story of Success*, Malcolm Gladwell takes a look at what factors lead to exceptional levels of success in a variety of fields, studying superachievers from Bill Gates to the Beatles. He comes to a startling conclusion: The key to success in any field is practicing a skill for ten thousand hours. His ten-

> **Oz Principle**
>
> *You unleash the power of personal accountability by asking yourself the right questions.*

thousand-hour rule suggests that extraordinary success happens not by chance or circumstance but by sheer practice and effort.

So be patient with your plans and remain consistent in your efforts to Do It. They will pay off. As actor Will Smith said, "The separation of talent and skill is one of the greatest misunderstood concepts for people who are trying to excel, who have dreams, who want to do things. Talent you have naturally. Skill is only developed by hours and hours and hours of beating on your craft."

A Word of Warning

Even though we've spent nearly thirty years eating, drinking, living, and sleeping accountability, we would be the first to tell you not to go overboard in your own journey toward greater accountability.

Don't Take Accountability to the Extreme

Though we'd like you to make a conscious effort to apply these principles, please don't take any of this too far. Don't beat yourself up when you slip now and then. Don't hold yourself responsible for anything that really does lie beyond your control. For example, you did not:

- choose the family into which you were born
- organize your own DNA on a molecular level
- set your own IQ
- dictate your native country or its political climate
- make a criminal or anyone else do something awful to you
- pick your boss or make her the big, lovable fuzz ball she is
- cause some destructive act of nature to descend on you or your home

Such circumstances are truly beyond your control. But that doesn't mean you aren't accountable for what you do about them now.

Practice Before You Preach

With your newfound knowledge about the power of personal accountability, you will be prompted to tell others about it. Sharing the lessons of personal accountability is a good thing, but it's hard to help others get Above The Line when you aren't there yourself. Just remember, it's not "Practice what you preach," it's "Practice before you preach." In our experience, when you do this, other people will see the positive changes in you and wonder what's in your water—what you've been doing. As you work with others and share what you've learned, you will help them escape their bad Below The Line habits while improving your own ability to remember these principles and make them part of your daily life.

Manage Your Stress

In your quest to live Above The Line and accomplish your goals, fix your problems, or set new records, you may be driven to overachieve in one way or another. That can get stressful. We all need to manage our stress. The right amount of stress is good, but when we overload, it makes us less effective.

Start by getting the sleep you need. Most people need eight hours of sleep but get only six and a half. Why does that affect our well-being? Scientists say that the last one and a half hours of sleep is when most of our rapid eye movement (REM) sleep occurs. REM is the periodic, jerky movement of the eyes that signals dreaming, which is essential to our mental equilibrium and memory. Missing that last hour and a half also increases the chance of anxiety and depression—two challenges that plague society today. Getting the optimal amount of sleep naturally enhances our levels of dopamine and serotonin, hormones that trigger happy feelings. If you miss the sleep, you decrease your happiness hormones and increase your risk of having to run to the doctor—and most medications for anxiety and depression offer only a slight bump in dopamine and serotonin levels anyway. We aren't saying that depression isn't a very real condition that often lies outside one's control and requires serious medical intervention. We're just saying that getting the right amount of sleep is something you can control. And should.

Bottom line: Enough sleep, regular exercise, and healthy eating can work more wonders than all the drugs in the world. Be sure to pay attention to the basics. They matter.

Lift Others Above The Line

We once heard a story about a small group of men who were asked to move a large piano from one room to another in their local church. Grand pianos are big, heavy, clumsy, and valuable, and none of these amateur movers knew how to pull it off. A number of ideas popped up as to how to do it, but none of them seemed to guarantee the safety of the men or the piano. Then someone suggested they all just stand close and "lift where you stand." This seemed way too simple, but when the men tried it, the piano rose into the air and moved as if by magic. After a lot of talk and failed ideas, these men discovered that they just needed to stand together and *lift where they stood*.

We think accountable people do the same thing whenever they cross paths with someone they are connected with who is stuck Below The Line. While reading this book, you have probably been saying to yourself, *Wow, so-and-so could really use this advice.* We all know someone who needs to escape the gravitational force Below The Line, probably someone we know quite well: a coworker, husband, wife, partner, in-law, relative, team member, boss, or friend.

Lifting others Above The Line requires that you help them apply the Steps To Accountability to their situation. First ask them, "What is the reality you most need to acknowledge?" Really listen and hear their concerns, which will likely be a flood of all the obstacles and bad things that stand in their way and keep them from moving forward. Be sure to help them see the whole picture, the true reality of the situation they face.

Then ask, "How are you contributing to the problem and/or solution?" Be sure they can make that all-important link to their role in what is happening.

Next comes the Solve It question: "What else can you do (to make progress, overcome the obstacle, or move forward)?" You may have to ask this question repeatedly. Some of the additional questions you learned earlier in this chapter could also be helpful here, such as "If your life depended on it, what else would you do?"

Oz Principle

Lift others Above The Line.

Finally ask, "What are you accountable to do and by when?" Laying out a concrete plan to move forward is a great way to end the conversation when you are lifting others Above The Line by helping them See It, Own It, Solve It, and Do It. It's an empowering gift you'll be giving them, one that instills hope and inspires the necessary steps to move forward. Remember that when you "lift where you stand" and help others to rise Above The Line— everyone benefits.

Keep Stepping!

Throughout this book we've mentioned Dorothy, the Scarecrow, the Tin Man, and the Cowardly Lion. We've reviewed their discoveries, how they learned what they needed to do and—with a little help now and then—got it *done*.

If a friend saw you reading this book and asked, "What is *The Wisdom of Oz*?" how would you respond? By now you know it's not about the Wizard, the yellow brick road, wicked witches, or flying monkeys. We hope you would answer that *The Wisdom of Oz* is about discovering the power of taking personal accountability for the things you want to do and the problems you want to solve. It's about taking the Steps To Accountability to See It, Own It, Solve It, and Do It and being filled with the knowledge and desire to stay Above The Line. It's about overcoming your circumstances and not being overcome by them. In the end, it's about coming to the realization that only when you assume full accountability for your thoughts, feelings, actions, and results can you direct your own destiny; otherwise, someone or something else will.

It's worth repeating, *The Wisdom of Oz* is, above all, simply this:

Only you can unleash the positive power of personal accountability to overcome the obstacles you face and achieve the results you want.

We hope you now feel exhilarated over the possibility of applying *The Wisdom of Oz* and all its principles to every nook and cranny of your life. Armed with this wisdom, you should now feel prepared to move whatever mountains are in your way and go on to achieve your heart's desires. We've seen it done millions of times. We will see it done millions more and are confident you can do it too.

The beginning . . .

The WISDOM of OZ

THE OZ PRINCIPLES

W e thought it might be helpful to include a collection of all the *Oz Principles* we have presented throughout *The Wisdom of Oz*. Here they are in one place, so that you can quickly refresh your understanding of these keys to greater accountability.

CHAPTER 1

- When you can't control your circumstances, don't let your circumstances control you.

- Every break "through" requires a "break with."

- Greater accountability is the most powerful choice you will ever make.

CHAPTER 2

- Accountability is something you do to yourself.

- It's not wrong to go Below The Line; it's just not effective to stay there.

- Think Above The Line.

- You must be personally accountable for how you *think* and *act*.

CHAPTER 3

♦ Nothing much good happens Below The Line.

♦ Playing the blame game never brings better results. Never.

♦ Don't play the victim.

CHAPTER 4

♦ See things as they really are.

♦ Examine your blind spots.

♦ Seeing It often has more to do with your ears than your eyes.

♦ Accountable people seek feedback.

♦ Feedback creates accountable people.

CHAPTER 5

♦ Ask yourself, are you a "renter" or an "owner"?

♦ To Own It means to leave it better than you found it.

♦ Go the extra mile; it will make you stand out from the crowd.

♦ If you are not part of the problem, you can't be part of the solution.

♦ If you can't make the link, you don't Own It!

CHAPTER 6

♦ Look beyond the "quick fix."

♦ Think as if your life depended on it.

♦ You've got to move a lot of dirt to get the gold.

♦ Action often produces results, even if you don't know what you are doing.

CHAPTER 7

♦ Nothing great happens until you do something.

♦ You've got to want it more than you don't want it.

♦ Don't let gravity pull you down.

♦ Reasons become excuses as soon as you start using them to stop trying to solve the problem.

CHAPTER 8

♦ Make it happen!

♦ You can't be in two places at one time—choose to be Above The Line.

♦ The most important person to get Above The Line is you.

♦ You unleash the power of personal accountability by asking yourself the right questions.

♦ Lift others Above The Line.

The
WISDOM
_of_
OZ

Only you can unleash the positive power of personal accountability to overcome the obstacles you face and achieve the results you want.

ACKNOWLEDGMENTS

Our thanks go first to the millions of people who have been trained in the concepts and principles presented in this book. These folks have made *The Oz Principle* the most widely read business book on the topic of accountability. Without them *The Wisdom of Oz* would not have been possible.

To Adrian Zackheim and the entire Portfolio team, including Natalie Horbachevsky and Will Weisser, we offer deep appreciation for the enthusiasm and support they have shown for our work on accountability over the years. Their confidence in the principles we present has greatly contributed to the worldwide distribution and success of our books.

Special thanks go to David Pliler, who offered thoughtful and ongoing support to help shape this book. His creative talents and contributions are very much appreciated.

As always, we thank our longtime friend and collaborator Michael Snell, a great partner in our continuing work to spread the message of greater accountability.

Unquestionably, we could include many individuals without whose help and input we could not have created *The Wisdom of Oz*. This is not just a book; it is a collection of timeless principles of success that have been field tested for over two decades by all of our colleagues at Partners In Leadership. Thank you. Your contributions are immense. Special thanks to Pete Theodore for the tasteful artwork and design contributions.

Finally, we express our gratitude to our wives, Gwen and Becky, and to our families, who make it all worth it!

ABOUT THE AUTHORS

Three-time *New York Times* bestselling authors Roger Connors and Tom Smith have written more on the subject of personal accountability than anyone, ever. Known by many as "the Oz guys" based on their breakthrough bestseller, *The Oz Principle: Getting Results Through Individual and Organizational Accountability*, Roger and Tom have spent the last 25 years coaching and consulting some of the top business leaders and organizations in the world. They are the co-founders of Partners In Leadership, the Accountability Training and Culture Change Company. The leaders they have worked with have gone on to become industry superstars and are hailed as some of the most influential people in their areas of expertise, having had incredible impact on the quality of the lives of millions of people around the globe.

Considered "worldwide experts on the subjects of accountability and change," Roger and Tom's company has provided leadership training and conducted organizational transformations in thousands of organizations reaching millions of people. Their work has created billions of dollars of shareholder wealth, hundreds of thousands of jobs and has resulted in some of the best workplaces in the world. You can learn more about their books, workshops, and training by visiting

www.thewisdomofozbook.com.

DON'T STOP NOW

Take the next step and join the millions of business professionals who have already experienced the power of personal accountability and put *The Wisdom of Oz* to work in your business or organization.

Don't stop now. You'll be glad to know we have more tools available to help you create greater personal and organizational accountability at work—all at

www.thewisdomofozbook.com.

- ♦ **Where Do You Stand?** Evaluate yourself, your team, or even an entire organization on how well you demonstrate the Steps To Accountability and get your score for free.

- ♦ **Bestselling Books.** Dig deeper with any of our other *New York Times* bestselling books. Discover more on personal accountability (*The Oz Principle*), holding others accountable (*How Did That Happen?*), and creating a culture of accountability (*Change the Culture, Change the Game*).

♦ **Webinars and Workshops.** Put accountability to work in our free monthly webinars or open-enrollment public workshops.

♦ **Business Services.** Transform your team or organizational culture with our fully integrated Three Tracks To Creating Greater Accountability training, PILtools digital learning tools, and world-class facilitators and speakers.

Visit www.thewisdomofozbook.com to enjoy
even greater success at work.